Ten Thousand Steps in Her Shoes

MIDDLE EAST AND NORTH AFRICA
DEVELOPMENT REPORT

Ten Thousand Steps in Her Shoes

The Role of Public Transport in Women's Economic Empowerment

Muneeza Mehmood Alam and Lisa Bagnoli

Middle East and North Africa Development Report Series

This series features major development reports from the Middle East and North Africa region of the World Bank, based on new research and thoroughly peer-reviewed analysis. Each report aims to enrich the debate on the main development challenges and opportunities the region faces as it strives to meet the evolving needs of its people.

TITLES IN THE MIDDLE EAST AND NORTH AFRICA DEVELOPMENT REPORT SERIES

Ten Thousand Steps in Her Shoes: The Role of Public Transport in Women's Economic Empowerment (2024) by Muneeza Mehmood Alam and Lisa Bagnoli

Informality and Inclusive Growth in the Middle East and North Africa (2023) by Gladys Lopez-Acevedo, Marco Ranzani, Nistha Sinha, and Adam Elsheikhi

Exports to Improve Labor Markets in the Middle East and North Africa (2023) by Gladys Lopez-Acevedo and Raymond Robertson

Blue Skies, Blue Seas: Air Pollution, Marine Plastics, and Coastal Erosion in the Middle East and North Africa (2022) by Martin Philipp Heger, Lukas Vashold, Anabella Palacios, Mala Alahmadi, Marjory-Anne Bromhead, and Marcelo Acerbi

Distributional Impacts of COVID-19 in the Middle East and North Africa Region (2021) edited by Johannes G. Hoogeveen and Gladys Lopez-Acevedo

The Reconstruction of Iraq after 2003: Learning from Its Successes and Failures (2019) by Hideki Matsunaga

Beyond Scarcity: Water Security in the Middle East and North Africa (2018) by World Bank

Eruptions of Popular Anger: The Economics of the Arab Spring and Its Aftermath (2018) by Elena Ianchovichina

Privilege-Resistant Policies in the Middle East and North Africa: Measurement and Operational Implications (2018) by Syed Akhtar Mahmood and Meriem Ait Ali Slimane

Jobs or Privileges: Unleashing the Employment Potential of the Middle East and North Africa (2015) by Marc Schiffbauer, Abdoulaye Sy, Sahar Hussain, Hania Sahnoun, and Philip Keefer

The Road Traveled: Dubai's Journey towards Improving Private Education: A World Bank Review (2014) by Simon Thacker and Ernesto Cuadra

Inclusion and Resilience: The Way Forward for Social Safety Nets in the Middle East and North Africa (2013) by Joana Silva, Victoria Levin, and Matteo Morgandi

Opening Doors: Gender Equality and Development in the Middle East and North Africa (2013) by World Bank

From Political to Economic Awakening in the Arab World: The Path of Economic Integration (2013) by Jean-Pierre Chauffour

Adaptation to a Changing Climate in the Arab Countries: A Case for Adaptation Governance and Leadership in Building Climate Resilience (2012) by Dorte Verner

Renewable Energy Desalination: An Emerging Solution to Close the Water Gap in the Middle East and North Africa (2012) by World Bank

Poor Places, Thriving People: How the Middle East and North Africa Can Rise Above Spatial Disparities (2011) by World Bank

Financial Access and Stability: A Road Map for the Middle East and North Africa (2011) by Roberto R. Rocha, Zsofia Arvai, and Subika Farazi

From Privilege to Competition: Unlocking Private-Led Growth in the Middle East and North Africa (2009) by World Bank

The Road Not Traveled: Education Reform in the Middle East and North Africa (2008) by World Bank

Making the Most of Scarcity: Accountability for Better Water Management Results in the Middle East and North Africa (2007) by World Bank

Gender and Development in the Middle East and North Africa: Women in the Public Sphere (2004) by World Bank

Unlocking the Employment Potential in the Middle East and North Africa: Toward a New Social Contract (2004) by World Bank

Better Governance for Development in the Middle East and North Africa: Enhancing Inclusiveness and Accountability (2003) by World Bank

Trade, Investment, and Development in the Middle East and North Africa: Engaging with the World (2003) by World Bank

All books in the Middle East and North Africa Development Report series are available for free at https://openknowledge.worldbank.org/handle/10986/2168.

Contents

Maps

Tables

Foreword

Women across the globe face numerous mobility challenges. Transport provides many benefits that should be enjoyed equally by all users, regardless of gender or life circumstances. However, this use requires a paradigm shift in transport planning. By enabling women, men, girls, and boys from all walks of life to fulfill their mobility needs, transport planning can become an important instrument for not only promoting economic, political, and social equity but also for enabling people, cities, and countries to grow.

In the Middle East and North Africa (MENA) region, women's university enrollment surpasses men's, yet their labor force participation rate remains low and stagnant. What is preventing the women of MENA from translating their educational achievements into economic productivity? Is it a matter of personal preference or structural barriers, or both? This report examines one structural barrier to women's participation in the labor force—the public transport system—in the context of the cities of Amman, Jordan; Beirut, Lebanon; and Cairo, the Arab Republic of Egypt.

This report finds that many women express a "latent desire" to work but face transport-related barriers that, once addressed, can lead to significant economic gains. While the report reveals that issues of public transport affordability and accessibility are common to all three cities, it also identifies important tailored and concrete city-specific actions to enhance women's access to economic opportunities in urban MENA.

This work demonstrates that "one-size-fits-all-women" transport policies designed to benefit women may leave many of them behind. Tailored action is needed across and within cities, depending on the needs of the different women who use public transport.

Gender equity in transport use can be only partially accomplished through policy interventions, regardless of how well intentioned and progressive they may be. Public awareness and endorsement of the benefits of greater gender equality—within households, workplaces, and society at large—are as crucial to advancing women's participation in the economy as are policy reforms and the state, civil society, and corporate actions that protect the interests of women and other disadvantaged groups and facilitate their agency.

The analysis and recommendations presented in this report should help policy makers in Jordan, Lebanon, and Egypt design concrete actions, improve women's mobility through public transport, and create an enabling environment to increase their economic participation.

Ferid Belhaj
Vice President
Middle East and North Africa Region
World Bank

Acknowledgments

This report originated from a collaboration between the Middle East and North Africa (MENA) Transport Team and the MENA Chief Economist's Office in 2020.

The report has been prepared by a core team led by Muneeza Mehmood Alam, senior transport economist, and comprises Lisa Bagnoli, consultant; Tamara Kerzhner, consultant; and Mira Morad, senior transport specialist, from the MENA Transport Unit of the World Bank.

The team is grateful to Paul Noumba Um, regional director for infrastructure, MENA Region; Roberta Gatti, chief economist, MENA Region; Stefan G. Koeberle, director, strategy and operations, MENA Region; Jean-Christophe Carret, country director for the Islamic Republic of Iran, Iraq, Jordan, Lebanon, and Syria, MENA Region; Marina Wes, country director for the Arab Republic of Egypt, the Republic of Yemen, and Djibouti, MENA Region; and Ibrahim Dajani, practice manager, MENA Transport Unit, for their support and guidance. The team also thanks Rabah Arezki, former chief economist, MENA Region, and Olivier Le Ber, former practice manager, MENA Transport Unit, for guiding this work in the earlier stages.

The core team thanks peer reviewers Matias Herrera Dappe, Karla Dominguez Gonzalez, and Nato Kurshitashvili for their comments. Marian Arakelian and Melanie Jaya are thanked for administrative support. The team also thanks May Ibrahim for reviewing the final report.

The extended team for the report includes Lina Abdelghaffar, Hakim A. A. Al-Aghbari, Affouda Leon Biaou, Nazmul Chaudhury, Munyaradzi Chidakwa, Nobuhiko Daito, Nabeel Darweesh, Jonathan Davidar, Salma Abdel Fattah, Arturo Ardila Gomez, Zeina El Khalil, Susan Lim, Alexis Madelain, Elisabeth Maier, Clotilde V. Minster, Ashraf Al-Saeed, and Gaelle Samaha from the World Bank.

About the Authors

Muneeza Mehmood Alam is a senior transport economist in the MENA Transport Unit of the World Bank. Muneeza joined the World Bank in 2015, bringing more than 15 years' experience working on development issues. During her time at the World Bank, Muneeza has worked on diverse topics relating to transport and economic policy, particularly economic corridors and regional connectivity, railways, logistics, urban transport, gender and spatial inclusion, and electric mobility. She has a keen interest in understanding the mechanisms through which the economic and social benefits of transport investments can be maximized and more equitably distributed. Muneeza has previously worked in the global as well as the South Asia transport units of the World Bank. Before joining the World Bank, she worked in economic consulting. She holds a PhD in economics from Yale University.

Lisa Bagnoli was a consultant with the MENA Transport Unit of the World Bank at the time of this writing, where she primarily worked on transport policy and gender. She is currently in the Infrastructure and Energy Sector of the Inter-American Development Bank, where she focuses on issues related to transport, energy, and water and sanitation in Latin America and the Caribbean. Prior to joining the World Bank, Lisa focused her work and research on the social and distributional impacts of public policies in various sectors, including transport, energy, health, and labor markets. She has a strong interest in understanding the effects of policy reforms on the most vulnerable populations. Lisa holds a PhD in economics from the Université libre de Bruxelles and is an associate fellow at the European Center for Advanced Research in Economics and Statistics.

Executive Summary

Today, in the Middle East and North Africa (MENA) region, women have a higher university enrollment rate than men, yet their labor force participation (LFP)[1] rate remains low and stagnant. What is preventing these women from translating their educational achievements into economic productivity? Is it a matter of personal preference or structural barriers, or is it both? Although transport systems have been shown to play a significant role in women's participation in the labor force globally, this topic has been little explored in the MENA region.

STUDY PURPOSE, DATA, AND STATISTICAL ANALYSIS

This report examines the role of public transport in women's access to economic opportunities in urban MENA. It studies the links among mobility, gender, and access to economic opportunities and focuses on three metropolitan areas—Amman, Jordan; Beirut, Lebanon; and Cairo, the Arab Republic of Egypt.[2] These cities were chosen for their contrasting size, context, and economic stability. All three cities have a low LFP rate for women and a significant disparity between the LFP rates of men and women.

This report focuses on five aspects of the public transport system and their implications for men's and women's mobility choices and barriers:

- The availability of public transport close to households and employment;

- The accessibility to job opportunities through the public transport network;

- The affordability of public transport;

- The acceptability of using public transport given social and cultural norms; and

- The safety from crime and harassment when using public transport and its infrastructure.

The report reveals that a significant percentage of working-age women in Amman, Beirut, and Cairo want to be economically active but are constrained due to deficiencies in the transport system. In each city, many of the interviewed non-working women stated that the lack of affordable, comfortable, safe, time-efficient, and reliable transport options prevents them from looking for work. This finding corresponds to 6 in 10 women in Amman, 5 in 10 in Beirut, and 4 in 10 in Cairo (refer to figure ES.1).

Improving the public transport system can enable women to contribute significantly to the economy. Statistical analysis confirms that a well-functioning public transport system is crucial for enhancing women's LFP, but the most important constraints they face differ by city and income levels. For example, in Amman, improving the safety of public transport by 5 percentage points (pp) may increase the city's gross domestic product (GDP) by 2.3 percent if the additional women who are seeking work find employment. In Cairo, a 5-pp improvement in accessibility may increase the city's GDP by 0.8–1.6 percent if the additional women seeking work find employment.

The report builds on three types of data collected in each metropolitan area, all of which were collected in 2022. The first type is the transport network data for the complete public transport network in each metropolitan area, which is complemented by built environment safety audits to understand the characteristics of the public transport system. The second type is intercept surveys of public transport users (3,027 men and 2,806 women across the three cities) to understand their system utilization. The third type is a household survey (2,951 men and 2,961 women ages 18–50 across the three cities) to understand the overall mobility of the working-age population. The survey also includes many personal and community characteristics that influence the relationship between mobility and access to economic opportunities.

FIGURE ES.1

Role of Public Transport in Women's Economic Empowerment

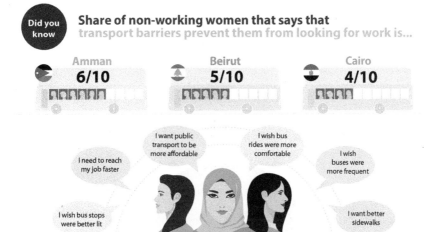

Did you know

Share of non-working women that says that transport barriers prevent them from looking for work is...

Amman	Beirut	Cairo
6/10	**5/10**	**4/10**

I want public transport to be more affordable

I wish bus rides were more comfortable

I need to reach my job faster

I wish buses were more frequent

I wish bus stops were better lit

I want better sidewalks

The Challenges

1 Percentage of women public transport users who face such problems

Amman
Uncomfortable	60%
Length of trips	42%
Waiting time	40%

Beirut
Road safety	58%
Too expensive	58%
Uncomfortable	49%

Cairo
Length of trips	35%
Waiting time	26%
Too expensive	25%

2 Percentage of total jobs reachable within 60 minutes by using public transport or walking

Amman 18%   Beirut 30%   Cairo 13%

The Potential | ## The Road Ahead

Improving public transport in MENA can encourage more women to seek economic opportunities, potentially yielding **GDP gains.**

Amman
2.3% potential increase in Amman's GDP.
If safety at public transport stops improves by 5 percentage points—59,000 more women will look for work.

Cairo
0.8%–1.6% potential increase in Cairo's GDP.
If accessibility through public transport improves by 5 percentage points—337,000 to 614,000— more women will look for work.

In Amman, Beirut, and Cairo, improving accessibility will increase the LFP among women from low-income households.

A well-functioning public transport system is necessary to improve women's economic participation in MENA.

This requires interventions that

Enhance the public transport network coverage, speed, affordability, and walkability of all cities

Develop customized solutions to improve public transport as one size does not fit all scenarios

Design complementary interventions in other sectors to create more opportunities for gainful employment of women

Source: Original figure for to this publication.
Note: GDP = gross domestic product; LFP = labor force participation; MENA = Middle East and North Africa.

SUMMARY OF THE FINDINGS

The findings of this report are summarized through a series of questions that build on each other. Together, these results demonstrate the importance of tailoring actions to context—a "one-size-fits-all-women" approach to improving the public transport system will leave many women behind, because it will not account for the unique circumstances and environments in which they operate.

The results also highlight the importance of intersectionality when focusing on women. For example, women in low-income households face specific challenges that would not be identified if only the average effect for all women had been investigated.

In addition, the study also emphasizes the need to go beyond transport to address other constraints that women may face, including gender norms, further underscoring the relevance of interinstitutional collaboration.

How Do Men's and Women's Mobility Patterns Differ Overall?

In the three cities covered by this report, men are more mobile than women. The gap between men's and women's mobility is greater in Amman and Beirut than in Cairo, where the average mobility is higher for both men and women. In Amman, only 53 percent of working-age women made at least one trip the day before the survey (a 16-pp gap with men); in Beirut, it was 56 percent (a 16-pp gap with men); and in Cairo, it was 90 percent (a 3-pp gap with men).

Among the men and women who are mobile, the mode of transport used differs significantly by city. In Amman and Beirut, private motorized transport is the dominant mode of travel for both men and women, whereas in Cairo, public transport is the dominant mode of travel, with taxis and call cabs a close second. This finding is reflected in the motorized vehicle ownership of households in the sample: 66 percent in Amman, 79 percent in Beirut, and 24 percent in Cairo.

In all three cities, men are much more reliant on private transport, and women rely on taxis and call cabs to meet their mobility needs, as evidenced by the share of men and women who hold a driver's license in the studied sample. In all three cities, men are much more likely than women to have a driver's license. The share of men and women who have licenses is lowest in Cairo. These results demonstrate that women in all three cities are likely to be more dependent than men on others (such as male household members driving them, taxis, or the equivalent) and on public transport to meet their mobility needs.

How Does the Use of Public Transport Vary between Men and Women?

Most men and women in Cairo use public transport, while only a minority do so in Amman and Beirut. Regardless, in all three cities, men are more likely than women to use public transport daily, even in Cairo, where women are more likely than men to use public transport overall.

Among public transport users, microbuses are the dominant means of transport used by both men and women in the three cities. Both spend almost an hour completing a trip by public transport in Amman and Cairo and three-quarters of an hour in Beirut. They also use multiple vehicles to complete a single trip, highlighting the importance of the feeder network and the coverage by public transport. In Amman, men and women use 1.8 and 1.9 vehicles, respectively, on their trip. This figure is more than in Cairo, which is 1.8 vehicles for men and 1.6 for women, and in Beirut, which is 1.4 vehicles for men and 1.3 for women.

In all three cities, work is the main reason for using public transport among men, while personal and other activities[3] are the main reasons for women. This difference is reflective of the division of labor within households.

Do Men and Women Report Facing the Same or Different Barriers to Using Public Transport? Are These Barriers the Same in Each City?

When using public transport, women face different challenges in each of the three cities, but the challenges faced by men and women within each city are, on average, similar. This finding affirms the notion that fundamental deficiencies in the public transport system can affect both men and women.

In Amman, the three main challenges for women using public transport are uncomfortable riding environments, long trip times, and long wait times. In Beirut, the three main challenges are road safety concerns, cost or affordability, and uncomfortable riding environments. In Cairo, the issues are long trip and wait times and cost or affordability.

Is Transport a Binding Constraint Preventing Women from Being Economically Active?

Essential differences exist in the commuting patterns of workers across the three cities. In Amman and Beirut, private vehicles constitute the main mode of transport, while in Cairo, public transport is the main transport mode. Among those who use public transport to commute to work, microbuses are the most used in Amman and Cairo, while buses or minibuses are the most used in Beirut.

Non-working women in all three cities express an openness to becoming gainfully employed if the conditions were favorable, indicating a "latent desire" to work. In all three cities, most non-working women say they would be willing to accept a job if it were available: 65 percent of non-working women in Amman, 59 percent in Beirut, and 67 percent in Cairo.

Among non-working women, many—62 percent of women in Amman, 52 percent in Beirut, and 48 percent in Cairo—identify commuting as a barrier to employment. When asked whether transport- or non–transport-related barriers constrain them, most women in all three cities indicate that transport-related barriers constrain them; a significant share also cite non–transport-related barriers, especially in Cairo. In Amman, 97 percent of women identify at least one transport-related constraint, while 14 percent identify at least one non–transport-related constraint. In Beirut, the figures are 97 percent and 16 percent, respectively, and in Cairo, the figures are 78 percent and 55 percent, respectively.

For transport-related constraints, women in Amman report commuting cost as the leading barrier to work, followed by trip length. This figure flips in Cairo, where trip length is the most reported barrier, followed by commuting cost. In Beirut, commuting cost is, by far, the dominant constraint. In terms of non–transport-related barriers, family preference that women do not work outside the home is the main non-transport barrier to commuting in Amman, while domestic duties are the main constraint in Beirut and Cairo.

How Much Can Improving the Public Transport System Enhance Women's Economic Participation?

Empirical measures of the accessibility, availability, and safety of public transport were constructed to assess how the spatial accessibility of jobs in each city, the availability of public transport near residential locations, and the safety at or near public transport stops affect the LFP of women as well as the likelihood of their employment.

All three cities have low accessibility levels to jobs by public transport and walking. On average, people in Amman can reach 18 percent of the total jobs in the metropolitan area in less than 60 minutes using public transport and walking; in Beirut, this figure is 30 percent, and in Cairo, a larger city, 13 percent. All three cities also have unequal access to public transport. Inequality in accessibility to jobs via public transport or walking is the highest in Amman, followed by Cairo and Beirut.

This measure of accessibility relates closely to transport type. In all three cities, as spatial access to jobs through public transport and walking improves, the reliance on public transport, walking and bicycling, and shared transport increases, whereas the reliance on private transport declines.

For safety and the built environment at or near public transport stops, poor pavement or sidewalks is the most salient issue in Amman and Cairo, whereas in Beirut, the lack of lighting at the stops is the most prevalent problem. Both aspects can affect the safety and security around public transport stops. Moreover, in Amman and Beirut, fewer women are present at transport stops than in Cairo.

Statistical analysis reveals that, in each of the three cities, women's LFP is differently influenced or constrained by the three spatial measures of public transport—accessibility, availability, and safety—and these constraints differ by income levels. In Amman, safety appears to be the most critical constraint women face, whereas spatial accessibility to jobs is more important for women from low-income households. A 5-pp increase in safety (from the composite safety index of 66 percent to 71 percent) is estimated to increase working-age women's LFP by 4.7 pp (from 13.6 percent to 18.3 percent). In practice, this figure corresponds to 59,000 additional women in the labor force in Amman.

In Beirut, we found no evidence that improving public transport availability, accessibility, or safety would significantly improve women's overall LFP. This finding may be due to the economic and financial crisis that Lebanon currently is facing that began in 2019 and was compounded by the Port of Beirut explosion in 2020. These crises have severely depressed the Lebanese economy and impacted available employment opportunities. However, evidence exists that spatial accessibility matters for women from low-income households.

In Cairo, both accessibility and availability of public transport appear to play an important role in determining women's LFP. A 5-pp increase in accessibility (from 13 percent to 18 percent) is estimated to increase working-age women's LFP by 4.9–8.9 pp (from 19.1 percent to 23.9–27.9 percent). In practice, these data correspond to 337,000–614,000 additional women in the labor force in Cairo. However, improving availability by 5 pp may increase women's LFP by 0.7 pp (52,000 additional women in the labor market).

Although accessibility, availability, and safety appear to affect women's likelihood of seeking a job to varying degrees, these measures seem to have little impact on women's subsequent employment probability. This finding is consistent with the idea that, while public transport is critical to improving women's access to employment opportunities, making women more likely to actively seek jobs, complementary actions are needed to translate this participation into gainful employment. Therefore, this finding represents missed opportunities both for women and cities overall.

Following the previous scenario, if all 59,000 additional women seeking a job in Amman were to find employment, on average, there would be a total extra income of more than (Jordanian dinar) JD 356 million per year (a 23 percent increase in Amman's GDP). Similarly, in Cairo, if all 337,000–614,000 women were to find employment, on average, it would lead to a total additional income of (Egyptian pounds) EGP 12.4 billion–EGP 22.7 billion per year (an 8–16 percent increase in Cairo's GDP).

What Concrete Actions Are Needed to Improve the Public Transport System?

This report reveals that, while some issues need to be addressed in all three cities, as common barriers and deficiencies exist, areas of improvements are specific to each city and context. In all three cities, affordability poses a major barrier to women commuting to work. Thus, lowering the cost of public transport or offering targeted fare concessions is needed. In addition, the overall low and unequal levels of accessibility of employment opportunities through public transport and walking highlight the need for the following concrete actions:

- Prioritizing public transport through integrated corridor management or the creation or improvement of mass transit;

- Improving existing land regulations to foster dense, diverse, and well-designed urban development; and

- Enhancing the walkability of the cities by improving sidewalks and walkways and developing pedestrian-first policies.

Some of the targeted concrete actions in each city could include the following:

- *Amman:* Providing a safe environment, such as well-lit and visible public transport stops and better walkways and bicycle paths. There is also a need for a code of conduct for public transport drivers and an easy mechanism to report gender-based violence, as well as to receive a swift response to these reports. To this end, Jordan adopted a code of conduct for public transport in January 2019 and has developed a mobile phone application that enables bus service users to report misconduct in the public transport system.

- *Beirut:* Enhancing the first and last mile coverage of, and comfort with, public transportation. There is also a need to enhance the lighting at public transport stops and to improve accessibility to them.

- *Cairo:* Expanding the availability of public transport near residential locations. This action requires reassessing the placement of public transport stops and increasing the frequency of public transport vehicles in addition to widening the network coverage of the public transport system.

What Else Is Needed to Enable Women's Active Employment in the Economy?

Although a good public transport system improves women's LFP, converting this participation into actual employment depends on many other factors, such as the labor market and environment, social, and household constraints, as well as gender norms and expectations about gender roles. For instance, there is a need to provide flexible work arrangements and supportive jobs that would allow women to balance their personal, family, and work lives, as well as protect them from gender-based discrimination,[4] and provide childcare options, such as high-quality day-care centers at or near where people work or live. Thus, along with improving the accessibility, availability, and safety of public transport, policy measures that address the work environment and social and household constraints are also needed.

NOTES

1. The *labor force participation rate* is the proportion of the population ages 15–64 that is economically active. This rate includes both people working and actively seeking work.
2. Throughout this Executive Summary and publication, all references to Amman, Beirut, and Cairo cover the entire metropolitan areas (also known as Greater Amman, Greater Beirut, and Greater Cairo) for the sake of conciseness.
3. These activities include social, medical, and care visits; accompanying someone else on their trip; and worship.
4. Some firms may have a business culture that does not value the contribution of their female staff or favors male employees to avoid providing maternity-related benefits or risking the loss of female employees after they are married.

Abbreviations

BRT	bus rapid transit
CTA	Cairo Transit Authority
GDP	gross domestic product
MENA	Middle East and North Africa
LFP	labor force participation
PP	percentage points

Units of currency

EGP	Egyptian pound
JD	Jordanian dinar
LP	Lebanese pound

CHAPTER 1

Introduction

BACKGROUND

The saying goes, "Real change happens one step at a time, yet discovering new horizons requires daring to lose sight of the land one walks on." In the context of women's economic empowerment, progress toward gender equality in the workforce may be slow and incremental. Yet, it also requires a willingness to take risks and challenge existing norms and systems. Nonetheless, the potential impacts of such efforts are both profound and significant. In this context, the role of transport emerges as a catalyst for transforming women's lives, enabling them to access economic opportunities, education, health care, and social activities.

Unfortunately, in many parts of the world, women face significant obstacles to mobility, limiting their access to the resources and services they need to thrive. Public transport has the potential to address these obstacles by providing safe, affordable, and reliable transport options that help women fully participate in their communities and realize their true potential.

Paradoxically, although today in the Middle East and North Africa (MENA) region more women than men enroll at university, the former's labor force participation (LFP) rate remains low and stagnant. The region has made remarkable strides in terms of women's life expectancy, infant mortality, and tertiary education. In some cases, women's performance in education has even led to a "reverse gender gap," with women outnumbering men in tertiary education. However, despite their educational attainment, women's economic participation across MENA countries remains low. Currently, 43 percent of women attend university in MENA, but only 21 percent participate in the labor force, as compared to 77 percent of men (refer to figure 1.1). While women's university enrollment has increased over the past decades, their LFP has remained low and stagnant over time (refer to figure 1.2). As compared with other regions, MENA exhibits the highest gender gaps in LFP and the lowest female LFP in absolute terms (refer figure 1.3).

How costly is it for MENA to rely on the talents of only half the population to achieve economic growth? The International Monetary Fund estimates that removing gender differences and equalizing LFP and hourly productivity between men and women would increase MENA's output by more than 50 percent (Ostry et al. 2018). However, various social and economic factors determine women's LFP at both the household and societal levels.[1] Some of these factors include cultural barriers, such as the social unacceptability of women working outside the home; the prioritization of men in or mixed workplaces; and structural barriers, such as a lack of childcare options, wage discrimination, and low wages (Arab Barometer 2023). Access to transport services is also emerging as a critical issue affecting women's decisions to participate in the labor market.

FIGURE 1.1

Current University Enrollment and LFP among Men and Women in the MENA Region

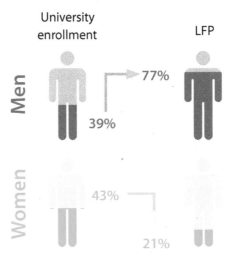

Source: Figure original to this publication using World Bank World Development indicators.
Note: LFP data are for 2019 and university enrollment data are for 2020. LFP = labor force participation; MENA = Middle East and North Africa.

FIGURE 1.2

University Enrollment and LFP of Women in the MENA Region, 1990–2020

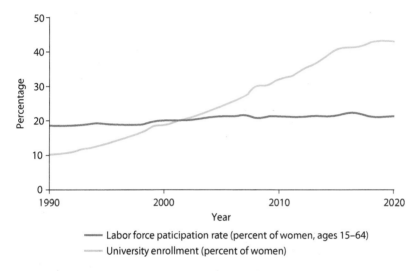

Source: Figure original to this publication using World Bank World Development Indicators.
Note: LFP = labor force participation; MENA = Middle East and North Africa.

Although transport systems have been shown to play a significant role in women's LFP globally, this topic has not been adequately explored in the MENA region (Alam et al. 2022). Extensive scientific and practitioner literature on the role played by gender in enabling or preventing people from accessing transport solutions has been evolving for decades (refer to box 1.1). Much evidence has been published in both developed and developing countries to demonstrate how gender inequities in transport access can create worse employment outcomes for women than for men (Ajibola, Komolafe, and Akangbe 2015; Cook and Butz 2018; Dobbs 2007; Seedhouse, Johnson, and Newbery 2016). The International Labor Organization (2017) has estimated that, in developing countries, limited access to and the safety of transport is the single greatest obstacle to women's participation in the labor market—it reduces their participation probability by as much as 16.5 percentage points.

Women's and men's experiences with transport systems differ significantly across all aspects of the travel experience. Factors influencing experience in the transport system can be classified as availability, affordability, spatial accessibility, safety, and acceptability

FIGURE 1.3

Gender Gaps in LFP, 1990–2019

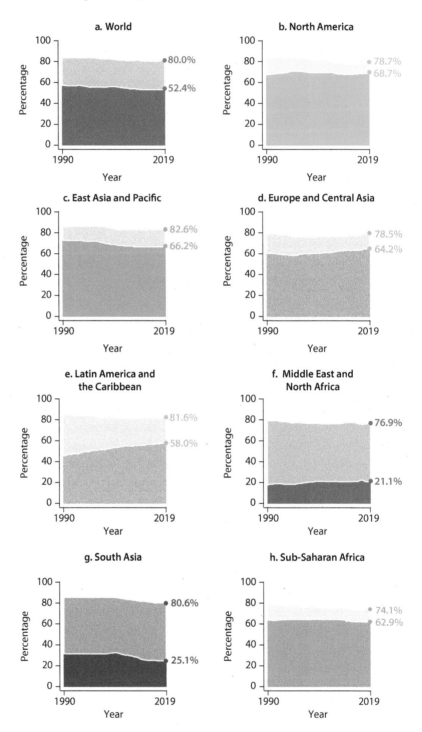

Source: Figure original to this publication using World Bank World Development Indicators.
Note: LFP = labor force participation.

BOX 1.1

Current Evidence on Gender, Mobility, and Access to Economic Opportunities

Women often face additional sociocultural constraints that exacerbate the adverse effects of poor public transport. Women's low financial capacity makes them more dependent on public transport than men, and the fare structure of multistop journeys (used more often by women) makes transport more expensive. The lack of personal security on public transport and around its infrastructure also disproportionally affects women, who might adjust their travel behavior for security considerations. As women spend more time on household responsibilities and multistop journeys, time-consuming public transport imposes a disproportionate burden on them and worsens their time poverty (Dominguez Gonzalez et al. 2020). Overall, unreliable, infrequent, and expensive public transport systems disproportionately burden women more than men, affecting their access to economic opportunities and essential services (Borker 2022).

Public transport systems also do not address the specific mobility needs of women. Typically, women constitute a lower share of travelers in public transport systems, but when they travel, they are more dependent on public transport than men (Borker 2022; Dominguez Gonzalez et al. 2020). Women tend to do more trip chaining and off-peak travel because they are more often in charge of domestic tasks and are responsible for the mobility of care. Mobility can pose barriers to women's social and economic empowerment. The availability, affordability, accessibility, social acceptability, and safety of public and private transport often influence women's ability to access education, jobs, health, social services, and recreation and leisure (Alam et al. 2022).

The limited evidence from Middle East and North Africa countries confirms that women constitute a sizable share of public transport users, but as this choice is often constrained, they are considered captive users. Women have lower access to private transport modes because they—especially when poorer—have less access to vehicles. They also bear the burden of indirect extra costs when using public transport caused by low accessibility and low affordability levels for women. These additional costs are akin to a "pink tax" on their mobility (Alam et al. 2021; Gatti et al. 2013; Minster et al. 2022).

Therefore, exploring women's mobility needs and constraints and how these can be addressed in the design of public transport systems is needed.

(Dominguez Gonzalez et al. 2020). However, a more recent systematic review of the global evidence on the topic has revealed that limited attention has been paid to gender differences in mobility in the MENA region (Alam et al. 2022; refer to map 1.1).

Can the lack of a well-functioning transport system explain the low levels of women's economic participation in MENA? Transport systems

MAP 1.1

Share of Scientific Literature on Gender and Mobility, by Region

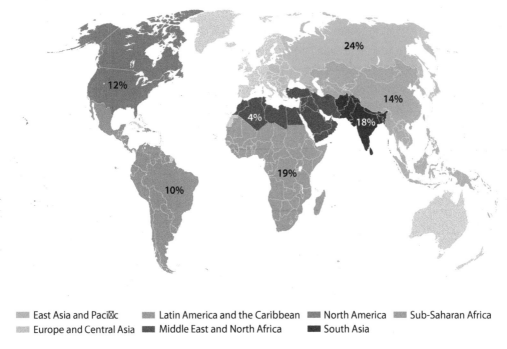

East Asia and Pacific	Latin America and the Caribbean	North America	Sub-Saharan Africa
Europe and Central Asia	Middle East and North Africa	South Asia	

Source: Alam et al. 2022.

can help ensure people reach their everyday destinations, such as jobs, schools, leisure activities, and health care facilities. Public transport services are the lifeline of transport networks because they are essential for people who are unable or do not want to drive, including those without access to personal vehicles—youth and older people, individuals with special needs, and middle- and lower-income individuals. Public transport is essential for the women of MENA regardless of their economic strata, given the wide gender gap in the possession of driver's licenses. Thus, public transport availability, affordability, and accessibility shapes how, when, and where women travel.

This publication sheds light on public transport's role in women's access to economic opportunities in urban MENA. The report examines the links among mobility, gender, and access to economic opportunities. It provides evidence of gender differences in mobility patterns and travel behavior, as well as the barriers and challenges women face when using public transport. This work also assesses whether deficiencies in the public transport system constrain women's economic participation.

This publication focuses on three metropolitan areas: Amman, Jordan; Beirut, Lebanon; and Cairo, the Arab Republic of Egypt (refer to box 1.2). These cities were chosen for their contrasting size, context, and economic stability. In doing so, the report does the following:

- Explores the links between mobility and gender and identifies women's barriers to using public transport, which requires an understanding of the characteristics of the public transport system itself—including transport means, network coverage, and service frequency. This work also requires a deep understanding of the mobility patterns of public transport users and their challenges.

- Examines the links among mobility, gender, and access to economic opportunities and identifies the barriers faced by working and nonworking women, which requires an understanding of the labor market

---

BOX 1.2

Transport and Economic Context in Amman, Beirut, and Cairo

The metropolitan area of the Greater Amman Municipality is a medium-size city with a low population density and a relatively stable economic situation. Mass transit services are emerging, but Amman still relies heavily on private vehicles. Its population reached 4.2 million in 2020, and its population density of about 5,000 inhabitants/km² is significantly lower than cities such as Beirut and Cairo. Amman houses most of Jordan's population, as the governorate of Amman (larger than the metropolitan area of Greater Amman) accounts for 42 percent of the country's population. The modal share of public transport is low in Amman, but mass transit services are emerging (for example, Phase 1 of the bus rapid transit is in soft operation).

The metropolitan area of Greater Beirut is a smaller city with multiple economic crises

and limited public transport infrastructure. The population of Greater Beirut was 2.2 million in 2016, with a density of about 11,000 inhabitants/km². Lebanon has weathered several crises for nearly 3 years that have depressed the Lebanese economy and affected available employment opportunities. Lebanese mobility is dominated by private vehicles, because the provision of public transport services is fragmented and unorganized, and infrastructure and facilities are limited and scarce (World Bank, forthcoming).

The metropolitan area of Greater Cairo is a vast and dense city, with many modes of mass and public transit. Greater Cairo is the largest urban area in the Middle East and North Africa, with a population of 21.75 million people and a density of about 12,000 inhabitants/km². The city has numerous means of public transport.

Sources: Morad et al. 2022; World Bank 2022; World Bank forthcoming.

aspirations and decisions of men and women. This work includes the mobility patterns of workers on their commuting trips and the reasons and barriers faced by those not working.

- Provides a model and estimation of the impact of various aspects of the public transport network on women's labor market outcomes, which requires an examination of how the availability of public transport close to residential locations, the accessibility of jobs throughout each city, and the safety at public transport stops affect women's LFP and their likelihood of being employed. By doing so, this report reveals whether improvements to public transport systems are necessary or a sufficient condition for enhancing women's economic empowerment.

CONCEPTUAL FRAMEWORK AND METHODOLOGY

Women's participation in the labor market depends on numerous factors. Their aspirations and ability to make decisions, as well as other individual characteristics such as educational and technical qualifications, can affect their choice to seek employment opportunities. This choice can also be constrained by external factors such as the country's legal environment or social norms, infrastructure and social services, and ease of using the public transport system, as well as the trade-offs between using public and private transport.

This publication focuses on the role that public transport systems play in enabling women to seek employment.[2] In doing so, it also covers aspects relating to the use of private transport modes. The report adopts an ecological framework to conceptualize how the transport system interacts with country-, community-, and individual-level factors in determining women's and men's mobility needs, choices, and access to economic opportunities (refer to figure 1.4).[3]

The transport system encompasses many components, including infrastructure design, operation, and transport services. This system interacts with country characteristics such as region, income, normative, legal, and policy context; community characteristics such as institutions, local, and community norms; and individual characteristics such as gender, age, personal income, family structure, responsibilities, and physical ability. These interactions can affect mobility needs and choices such as travel patterns and mode choices, including the choice between using private vehicles or public transport. All these factors are internalized and can shape women's aspirations and their decision about participating in the labor force, both under salaried employment or self-employment.[4] The decision to seek employment may lead to

FIGURE 1.4

Conceptual Framework for Women's Access to Economic Opportunities

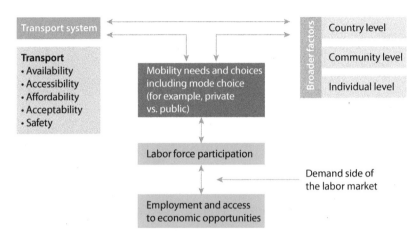

Source: Figure original to this publication using World Bank data.
Note: Men's access to economic opportunities can be similarly conceptualized; they typically face different broader factors and transport barriers than women. LFP = labor force participation.

actual employment, but it also depends on labor market factors such as the availability of jobs, flexibility of work, and absence of gender-based discrimination. Although the demand side of the labor market is an important determinant of women's labor market outcomes, it is not the primary focus of this report.

The report focuses on five main facets of the public transport system, which are defined as follows (Alam et al. 2022; Dominguez Gonzalez et al. 2020):

- *Availability* is the presence of public transport vehicles nearby, including both transport infrastructure and services. However, in urban settings, the availability of transport services may be more salient than the infrastructure. Availability might also be more salient for people who do not own private vehicles and instead rely solely on public transport to move around.

- *Accessibility* is the ease with which an individual can access opportunities (for example, employment) within the city space, depending on available transport infrastructure and services, personal characteristics, spatial distribution of economic opportunities, and other aspects.

- *Affordability* refers to the travel costs and the extent to which individuals have the means to travel to their destinations. It includes both the direct cost of the trip and the opportunity cost of other potential consumption that is foregone to make the mandatory trips. Therefore, the same trip might be affordable to one individual but not to another.

- *Acceptability* refers to social and cultural appropriateness, which includes the norms, judgments, attitudes, and behavioral reactions to women and men when they travel and use various means of transport.

- *Safety* refers to personal security from crime, freedom from harassment, and the perception of security when using transport. For women, other factors can influence their perceptions of security on public transport, including issues related to comfort, such as the crowdedness of vehicles or the lighting at a station, which might be closely related to the risks of harassment and the overall perception of personal security.

Understanding how improving the public transport system can contribute to women's economic empowerment requires a three-pronged approach:

- First, a thorough understanding of the characteristics of the public transport system itself is needed, including the means of public transport and available vehicles, the network coverage, and the service frequency.

- Second, a detailed understanding is required of the usage of the public transport system, the nature of trips made by public transport users, and the main challenges they experience.

- Third, an extensive understanding of how mobility through the public transport system fits within people's overall mobility choices and economic and social aspirations is necessary.

The three types of data collected for the report in each metropolitan area align with this three-pronged approach:

- The first data set collected is the transit network data for the complete public transport network in each metropolitan area and is complemented by built environment (safety) audits to understand the characteristics of the public transport system. These audits are conducted at public transport stops to assess safety level.

- The second data set collected is the intercept surveys of public transport users (3,027 men and 2,806 women across the three cities) to understand their system utilization.

- The third data set collected is a household survey to understand the overall mobility of the working-age population (2,951 men and 2,961 women, ages 18–50 across the three cities), as well as many personal and community characteristics that influence the relationship between mobility and access to economic opportunities.[5]

The final number of surveys collected in each city is summarized in figure 1.5.

The remaining chapters of this report are structured as follows:

- Chapter 2, which focuses on the links between mobility and gender in Amman, Beirut, and Cairo, provides a descriptive overview of the current transport systems, mobility patterns, and challenges identified by the population.

- Chapter 3, which examines the interplay among mobility, gender, and access to economic opportunities, adds to the previous discussion by including aspirations and labor market considerations.

FIGURE 1.5

Summary of Collected Data

Source: Figure original to this publication using World Bank data.

- Chapter 4 provides concrete recommendations for improving women's mobility and economic participation.

The findings of this work can be used to develop tailored actions to address the public transport barriers faced by women. Taken together, the evidence presented in this report illuminates one structural barrier that may be preventing women from participating in the labor force—the public transport system.

NOTES

1. Factors affecting women's decisions and ability to engage in the labor market include the level of economic development of cities, institutional settings, individual educational attainment, and social dimensions such as norms regarding women's roles within and outside the household.
2. *Employment* includes both salaried employment and self-employment.
3. This framework is adapted from Dominguez Gonzalez et al. (2020) and Alam et al. (2022).
4. The report covers both salaried employment and self-employment. In this context, the term *labor market* is used to include both.
5. All data were collected between May and November 2022, except for the public transport user surveys in Cairo, which was conducted in early 2021 as part of the Cairo Mobility Assessment and Public Transport Improvement Study (World Bank 2022). See Alam, Bagnoli, and Kerzhner (2023) for more details on the sampling methodology.

REFERENCES

Ajibola, B. O., S. E. Komolafe, and J. A. Akangbe. 2015. "Constraints Faced by Women Vegetable Farmers in Kwara State, Nigeria and Its Agricultural Practices." *Jordan Journal of Agricultural Sciences* 11 (4): 995–1005.

Alam, M. M., L. Bagnoli, and T. Kerzhner. 2023. "The ABCs of the Role That Public Transport Plays in Women's Economic Empowerment." Policy Research Working Paper 10404, World Bank, Washington, DC. http://hdl.handle.net/10986/39682.

Alam, M. M., M. Cropper, M. Herrera Dappe, and P. Suri. 2021. "Closing the Gap: Gender, Transport, and Employment in Mumbai." Policy Research Working Paper 9569, World Bank, Washington, DC. doi:10.1596/1813-9450-9569.

Alam, M. M., N. Kurshitashvili, K. Dominguez Gonzalez, K. Gonzalez Carvajal, and B. Baruah. 2022. *Is a Mile for One a Mile for All? A Knowledge Synthesis Report on Gender and Mobility (2000–20)*. Washington, DC: World Bank. doi:10.1596/37354.

Arab Barometer. 2023. *MENA Women in the Workforce 2022—Wave VII*. 2022 Arab Barometer Insight. https://www.arabbarometer.org/2023/02/mena-women-in-the-workforce/.

Borker, G. 2022. "Constraints to Women's Use of Public Transport in Developing Countries, Part I: High Costs, Limited Access, and Lack of Comfort." Global Indicator Brief No. 9, World Bank, Washington, DC. http://hdl.handle .net/10986/37821.

Cook, N., and D. Butz. 2018. "Gendered Mobilities in the Making: Moving from a Pedestrian to Vehicular Mobility Landscape in Shimshal, Pakistan." *Social & Cultural Geography* 19 (5): 606–25. doi:10.1080/14649365.2 017.1294702.

Dobbs, L. 2007. "Stuck in the Slow Lane: Reconceptualizing the Links between Gender, Transport and Employment." *Gender, Work & Organization* 14 (2): 85–108. doi:10.1111/j.1468-0432.2007.00334.x.

Dominguez Gonzalez, K., A. L. Machado, B. Bianchi Alves, V. Raffo, S. Guerrero, and I. Portabales. 2020. *Why Does She Move? A Study of Women's Mobility in Latin American Cities.* Washington, DC: World Bank. https://documents1. worldbank.org/curated/en/276931583534671806/pdf/Why-Does-She -Move-A-Study-of-Womens-Mobility-in-Latin-American-Cities.pdf.

Gatti, R., M. Morgandi, R. Grun, S. Brodmann, D. Angel-Urdinola, J. M. Moreno, D. Marotta, M. Schiffbauer, and E. Mata Lorenzo. 2013. *Jobs for Shared Prosperity: Time for Action in the Middle East and North Africa.* Washington, DC: World Bank. http://hdl.handle.net/10986/13284.

International Labor Organization. 2017. *World Employment and Social Outlook: Trends for Women 2017.* ILO. https://www.ilo.org/global/research /global-reports/weso/trends-for-women2017/lang--en/index.htm.

Minster, C., L. Ait Bihi Ouali, L. DiDomenico, and M. M. Alam. 2022. *Gendered Economic Impacts of Mobility in the MENA Region: A Literature Review.* Unpublished manuscript. World Bank, Washington, DC.

Morad, M., A. Ardila Gomez, H. A. A. Al-Aghbari; M. M. Alam, Y. Li, N. Daito, G. Samaha, O. E. Diaz, M. J. Sala Pelufo, and S. A. A. O. Aloul. (2022). *Jordan Public Transport Diagnostic and Recommendations (English).* World Bank, Washington, DC. http://documents.worldbank.org/curated/en /099825106052213281/P17389502814af03b0a85e0a27bbbbaa260.

Ostry, J. D., J. A. Alvarez, R. A. Espinoza, and C. Papageorgiou. 2018. "Economic Gains from Gender Inclusion: New Mechanisms, New Evidence." IMF Staff Discussion Note SDN/18/06. https://www.imf.org/en/Publications/Staff -Discussion-Notes/Issues/2018/10/09/Economic-Gains-From-Gender -Inclusion-New-Mechanisms-NewEvidence-45543.

Seedhouse, A., R. Johnson, and R. Newbery. 2016. "Potholes and Pitfalls: The Impact of Rural Transport on Female Entrepreneurs in Nigeria." *Journal of Transport Geography* 54: 140–47. doi:10.1016/j. jtrangeo.2016.04.013.

World Bank. 2022. "Green Transition of Transport in Egypt: Updates from Greater Cairo Mobility Assessment and Public Transport Improvement Study (MAPTIS)." Presentation. World Bank, Washington, DC. https://events .wbgkggtf.org/sites/kggtf_events/files/session/KGID_Greater%20Cairo%20 MAPTIS%20Overview.pdf.

World Bank. Forthcoming. *Lebanon Public Transport Diagnostic and Recommendations.* Washington, DC: World Bank.

CHAPTER 2

Mobility and Gender

BACKGROUND

Gender, along with social, economic, and cultural factors, remains a strong determinant of mobility choices and constraints. Despite making immense gains in education and employment, women across socioeconomic strata experience a wage gap when compared with men. This issue can influence women's choice of transport because of both affordability and safety. In addition, despite men's growing contributions to caregiving and social reproduction, women continue to bear disproportionate responsibilities for household and community maintenance, as well as reproduction.

What are women's most significant constraints when using different public and semi-private transport modes? What are the critical areas for improvement? Are the constraints that women and men face and their identified areas of improvement similar or different? This chapter answers these questions in the context of urban Amman in Jordan, Beirut in Lebanon, and Cairo in the Arab Republic of Egypt. The chapter explains the overall mobility patterns of the population using household surveys and then presents the characteristics of the public transport networks in the three metropolitan cities and their relative use in meeting their population's mobility needs. It uses the intercept surveys of public transport users to highlight the experiences of public transport users to understand their travel patterns and behaviors[1] and to identify the most important challenges they face and areas for improvement. By doing so, this chapter offers an understanding of how women's mobility can be improved.

OVERALL MOBILITY PATTERNS

This section illuminates the overall mobility patterns in Amman, Beirut, and Cairo.

Overall Mobility

Rapid urbanization across the globe has increased the demand for mobility.

How Mobile Are Men and Women in Their Daily Lives?

In each city, men are more likely than women to make at least one trip on a typical day. These gaps are wider in Amman and Beirut than in Cairo. In Amman, 69 percent of men and 53 percent of women made at least one trip on the day prior to the survey. These figures are similar in Beirut, with 72 percent of men and 56 percent of women making at least one trip. In Cairo, however, mobility is higher for both men and women, with 93 percent of men and 90 percent of women having made at least one trip (refer to figure 2.1).

What Transport Modes Are Used by Those Who Travel?

The transport modes used by individuals who travel differ by city. In Amman and Beirut, private motorized transport is the dominant mode of travel for both men and women, while in Cairo, public transport is the dominant mode of travel (with taxis and call cabs being a close second).

FIGURE 2.1

Share of the Population That Made at Least One Trip on the Day Prior to the Survey in Amman, Beirut, and Cairo, by Gender

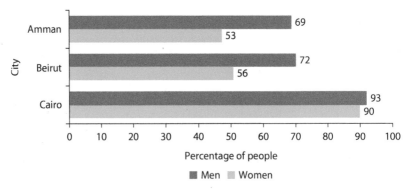

Source: Figure original to this publication using World Bank data: Household surveys.

Regardless of the city, men are more likely than women to use a private vehicle. In Amman and Beirut, the use of private vehicles is widespread, with more than half the population who had traveled the day before reportedly using a private vehicle. In Cairo, however, only 21 percent of men and 9 percent of women relied on a private vehicle (refer to figure 2.2). Regardless of location, men are more likely than women to use private motorized modes, while women are more likely than men to rely on taxis or call cabs.

The use of public transport also varies across cities, with lower percentages in Amman and Beirut as compared with Cairo. On a typical day in Beirut, only 7 percent of men and 6 percent of women who need to travel use public transport. These figures are twice as high in Amman, where 13 percent of both men and women use public transport. However, these percentages are very low when compared with Cairo, where 40 percent of men and 37 percent of women who travel use public transport on a typical day. During our survey period, the majority of respondents reported that their travel needs did not change due to the COVID-19 pandemic (refer to box 2.1).

FIGURE 2.2

Share of Men and Women Using Various Modes of Transport on the Day Prior to the Survey in Amman, Beirut, and Cairo

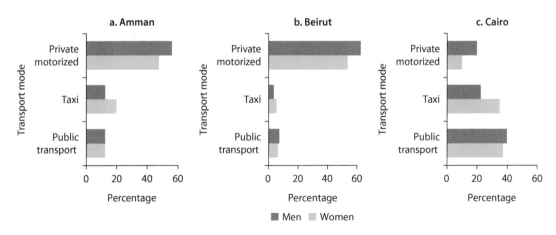

Source: Figure original to this publication using World Bank data: Household surveys.
Note: This figure is based on the percentages of men and women who used each means of transport on the previous day, provided they had made at least one trip on that day prior to being surveyed. Respondents may have used multiple modes of transport, but if they utilized two modes within the same category (such as car and motorcycle, or metro train and microbus), they were counted only once within that category.

BOX 2.1

Has the COVID-19 Pandemic Affected Men's and Women's Mobility in Amman, Beirut, and Cairo?

How different were the mobility patterns of the individuals prior to the COVID-19 pandemic? People who answered the household survey were asked whether their mobility needs and patterns had changed due to the pandemic. For most of respondents, their travel needs did not change. On average, individuals in Amman and Beirut report slightly more than in Cairo that their travel needs are different because of the pandemic (27 percent of both men and women in Amman, 31 percent of men and 34 percent of women in Beirut, and 16 percent of men and 14 percent of women in Cairo).

Only a small number of people report having changed the type of transport used because of the pandemic (refer to figure B2.1.1). This figure is higher in Amman and Beirut (9 percent of men and 7 percent of women in Amman; 6 percent of both men and women in Beirut) than in Cairo (3 percent of men and 2 percent of women).

FIGURE B2.1.1

Share of the Population in Amman, Beirut, and Cairo That Increased the Use of a Specific Type of Transport Because of the Pandemic, by Gender

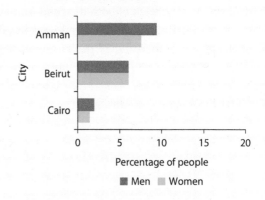

Source: Figure original to this publication using World Bank data: Household surveys.

Private Vehicle Ownership and Driver's Licenses

In all three cities, cars are the primary type of private vehicle owned by households, but the percentages of households that own a car are much higher in Amman and Beirut than in Cairo. Significant differences exist across cities. In Amman, 66 percent of households own a car but do not own any other type of vehicle such as bicycles or motorcycles. In Beirut, more households, 72 percent, own a car, and a minority of households also own other vehicles (16 percent own a motorcycle, and 4 percent own a bicycle). In Cairo, only a minority, 15 percent, of households own a car. An even smaller number own bicycles (2 percent) or motorcycles (9 percent) (refer to figure 2.3).

FIGURE 2.3

Private Vehicle Ownership in Amman, Beirut, and Cairo, by Type

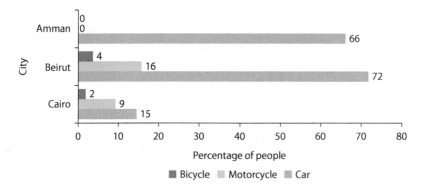

Source: Figure original to this publication using World Bank data: Household surveys.

Men are much more likely than women to have a driver's license. In Amman, almost 70 percent of men have a license as compared with 42 percent of women. Beirut has the highest share of people with a driver's license and is the only city where more than half the women sampled have a license (82 percent of men and 55 percent of women). In Cairo, the share of people with a driver's license is much lower than in the other two cities. Cairo also has the biggest gender difference: men (24 percent) are four times more likely to have a driver's license than women (6 percent) (refer to figure 2.4).

Globally, the number of men with driver's licenses far exceeds the number of women who have them, and women tend to travel by car more often as passengers than as drivers (Elias, Benjamin, and Shiftan 2015). While the women in the sample are less likely than men to have a driver's license, the high share of women having a license in absolute terms is indicative of the deficiencies in the public transport system. Thus, are women more likely than men to depend on others and public transport to meet their mobility needs?

PUBLIC TRANSPORT NETWORKS AND THEIR USE

This section discusses public transport networks and their use in Amman, Beirut, and Cairo.

· FIGURE 2.4

Driver's License Possession among Men and Women in Amman, Beirut, and Cairo

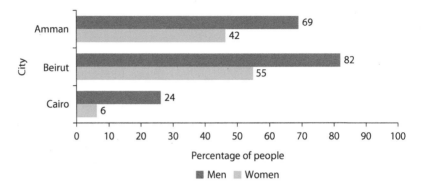

Source: Figure original to this publication using World Bank data: Household surveys.

Available Public Transport

Of the three cities, Cairo has the most public transport means available, followed by Amman, while Beirut has the fewest (refer to map 2.1). The public transport network for all three cities was mapped (refer to box 2.2).

In Cairo, the public transport network consists of the metro trains, buses or minibuses, and microbuses. In particular, buses are operated either by the Cairo Transit Authority (CTA) Bus[2] or other private bus companies.[3] The CTA also operates minibuses. Other minibuses include the CooP minibuses in Cairo. Finally, microbuses include privately owned 14-seaters and smaller Suzuki vans (unregulated 7-seaters), which operate short express routes with high frequency (World Bank 2022).

In Amman, public transport consists of buses, minibuses (coasters),[4] and services (owner-operated shared taxis running on fixed routes). The buses include the following three catagories: (a) Amman bus rapid transit (BRT), which are modern buses currently running on the existing BRT corridor; (b) Amman Bus, which was created by Amman Vision Transport as a high-quality bus system (Comprehensive Multiple Transportation Company, in a joint venture with the Turkish company Gürsel, holds the tender to operate Amman Bus); and (c) large buses, which are in a heterogeneous category that accommodates multiple operators, including individual private operators. Minibuses or coasters are owner-operated microbuses running on fixed routes and connecting the city center with the main commercial and residential areas. Services are owner-operated, shared taxis running on fixed routes, often functioning as a last-mile solution between large transport hubs and peripheral regions (Morad et al. 2022).

In Beirut, the public transport network consists of buses and minivans[5] (services and taxis are not included, because these operate as nearly door-to-door).[6] There are only a few government-owned buses in the city (owned and operated by the Railway and Public Transport Authority, also called *Office des Chemins de Fer et des Transports en Commun*), while the remaining buses and minivans are privately owned and operated.

Proximity of Public Transport Stops to Residential Locations

Bringing people and opportunities closer allows cities to prosper. Proximity to public transport stops is essential for people, especially in the middle and lower classes, to use affordable transport options. The frequency of public transport at the stop, the suitability of the route, and

MAP 2.1

Public Transport Network in Amman, Beirut, and Cairo

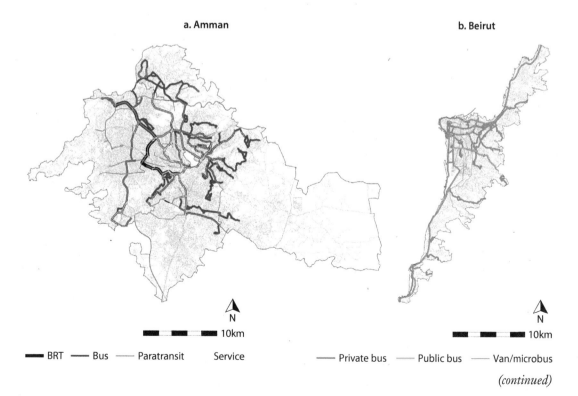

a. Amman   b. Beirut

N   N
10km   10km

■ BRT   — Bus   — Paratransit   Service   — Private bus   — Public bus   — Van/microbus

(continued)

MAP 2.1

Public Transport Network in Amman, Beirut, and Cairo (*continued*)

c. Cairo

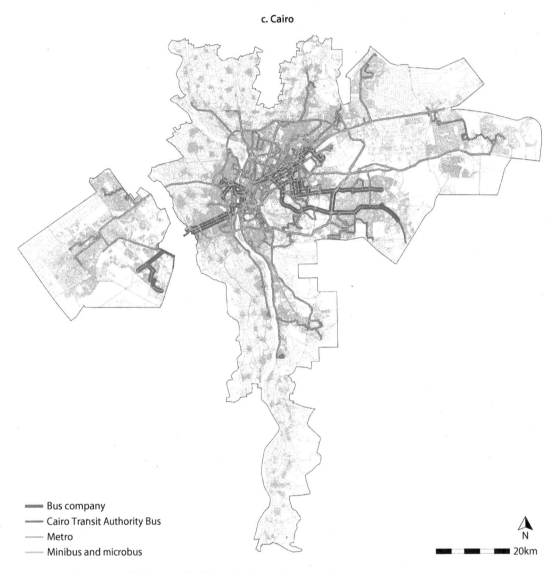

- ▬▬ Bus company
- ━━ Cairo Transit Authority Bus
- ── Metro
- ── Minibus and microbus

N

▰ ▰ ▰ 20km

Source: Map original to this publication using World Bank data: Transit network mapping.
Note: In Amman, the *bus rapid transit* is a type of bus; *paratransit* is equal to microbuses or coasters. In Cairo, a *bus company* aggregates three categories, while *minibus and microbus* aggregate five categories (including minibuses operated by the Cairo Transit Authority).

personal preferences also play a crucial role in determining an individual's preferred commuting mode.

Evidence suggests that, on average, people are willing to walk up to 400 meters to access local public transport stops; this distance translates to 5 minutes of walking time (Tennøy, Knapskog, and Wolday, 2022; van Soest, Tight, and Rogers, 2020). Thus, 5 minutes is the threshold of time

---

BOX 2.2

Methodology Used for Public Transport Network Mapping in Amman, Beirut, and Cairo

Transport network mapping includes all route-based public transport in Amman, Beirut, and Cairo. In each city, all fixed route-based public transport means were surveyed for the network mapping.[a] The mapping of the public transport system started with the collection of official routes and related information from government entities. Known gaps within these official records were filled in through desk research. Finally, a team of enumerators was deployed to map the actual routes and capture attributes such as frequency and fares using a mobile-based application. The building blocks of the fieldwork were public transport stations. Enumerators then conducted station surveys to identify all

routes departing from a specific station. This work resulted in a complete list of routes for the city for an assessment of the full extent of the transport network.

The routes were then traveled in both directions to map them. Any additional stations discovered through this method were also included using the above-mentioned process. These data not only contain the routes of the transport network but also provide information on the frequencies and timetables that were used to construct various indicators (refer to chapter 3). Frequency data were collected by interviewing passengers, drivers, and station managers. Map 2.1 illustrates the public transport network for each city.

a. *Route-based public transport* is defined as routes that have a fixed origin and destination and travel through key defined landmarks along the route.

---

that people are willing to walk to access local public transport before they start using private transport due to a long walking time.[7]

How Far Do People Walk to Reach a Public Transport Stop?

The three cities differ by how long people walk to reach a public transport stop (refer to figure 2.5). Public transport stops are closer to residential locations in Cairo than in Beirut and Amman. In Amman, only 23 percent of people have access to public transport in less than 5 minutes of walking, while 36 percent people have access in Beirut and 41 percent in Cairo.

Considering a 10-minute threshold, the percentage of people who can reach a public transport stop is 57 percent in Amman, 70 percent in Beirut, and 82 percent in Cairo. These figures also mean that the share of people walking for a long time (more than 20 minutes) to reach public transport can be as high as 16 percent in Amman, 10 percent in Beirut, and only 4 percent in Cairo.

FIGURE 2.5

Time to Reach a Public Transport Stop by Walking from Home in Amman, Beirut, and Cairo

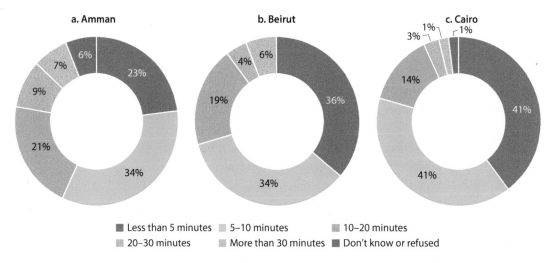

Source: Figure original to this publication using World Bank data: Household surveys.

Note: In Amman, public transport includes bus or minibus, microbus, and services; in Beirut, it includes bus or minibus and microbus; in Cairo, it includes metro trains, bus or minibus, and microbus.

How Does Proximity to Public Transport Stops Vary by Means of Transport?

The proximity of transport stops to residential locations varies greatly across transport means in Cairo, is less in Amman, and is almost none in Beirut (refer to figure 2.6). In Amman, service stops tend to be closer to residential locations than buses, minibuses, or microbuses (31 percent of households can reach a service in less than 5 minutes, while for microbuses, this figure is 14 percent). Amman also has a high percentage of people who do not know the location of transport stops.

In Beirut, there is almost no difference in the proximity of stops across transport means. In Cairo, most households are located at least 30 minutes from a metro station, while 80 percent are less than 10 minutes from a microbus stop. For buses and minibuses, it takes 10 minutes or less for 56 percent of the population to reach a transport stop.

How Often Do Men and Women Use Public Transport?

In Amman and Beirut, only a minority of the population uses public transport, whereas in Cairo, a large majority of the population relies on it. Men are more likely than women to use public transport daily, even in

FIGURE 2.6

Time to Walk from Home to a Public Transport Stop in Amman, Beirut, and Cairo, by Means of Public Transport

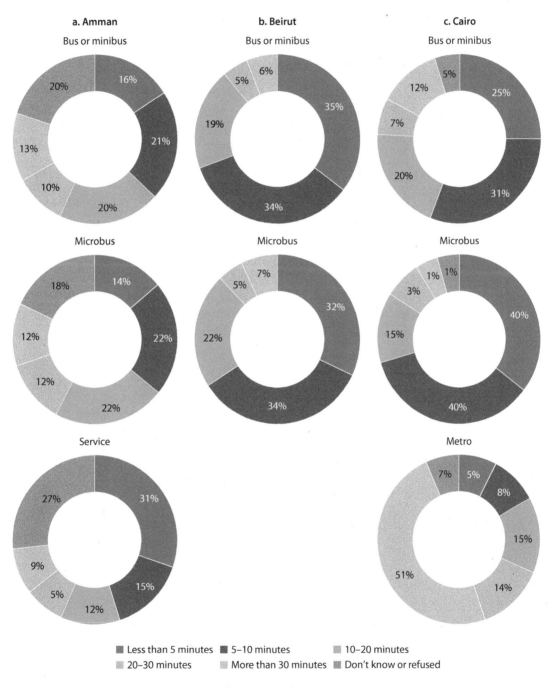

Source: Figure original to this publication using World Bank data: Household surveys.

Cairo, where women are more likely to use public transport overall. The distribution of the frequency of use of public transport varies across cities (refer to figure 2.7).

In Amman, the majority of the population (59 percent of men and 65 percent of women) does not use public transport. Women (35 percent) are less likely than men (41 percent) to use public transport. Among those who do use public transport, women (7 percent use it every day) are also less likely than men (15 percent use it every day) to use it very frequently.

In Beirut, 75 percent of the population never uses public transport. There is almost no difference between men and women, and among those who use public transport, the frequency is similar among men and women, and very few use it every day.

In Cairo, a large majority of people use public transport. This percentage is even larger for women (89 percent) than for men (85 percent), but women use it less frequently, with the share of women who use public transport daily being half of that of men.

Does the Frequency of Use Vary by the Means of Public Transport?

In Amman and Beirut, there is not much difference in the frequency of use among the various means of transport. In Cairo, however, most of the population uses microbuses, more than 50 percent uses the metro, and less than 40 percent uses buses or minibuses (refer to figure 2.8).

FIGURE 2.7

Frequency of Use of Public Transport in Amman, Beirut, and Cairo, by Gender

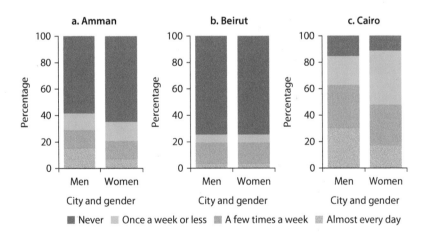

Source: Figure original to this publication using World Bank data: Household surveys.
Note: In Amman, public transport includes the bus or minibus, microbus, and services; in Beirut, transport includes the bus or minibus and microbus; and in Cairo, it includes metro trains, bus or minibus, and microbus.

FIGURE 2.8

Frequency of Use of Public Transport in Amman, Beirut, and Cairo, by Means of Public Transport

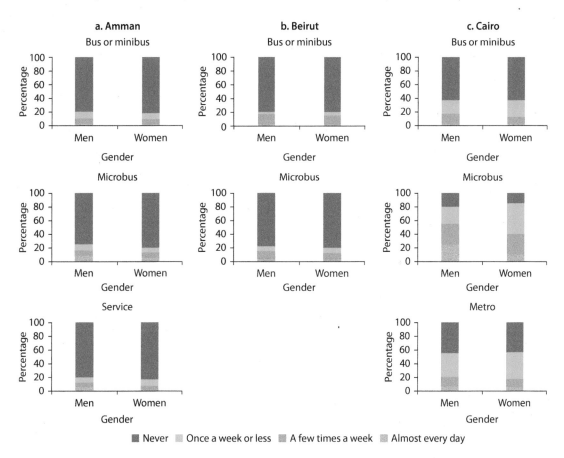

Source: Figure original to this publication using World Bank data: Household surveys.

PUBLIC TRANSPORT USERS

This section presents an in-depth analysis of the public transport user experience using interviews and surveys of public transport users at select public transport stops and surrounding areas. It describes the travel behaviors of public transport users, as well as the purpose, length, cost, and mode of the trips.

For What Reasons Do Men and Women Use Public Transport?

In the three cities, work is the main reason for using public transport among men. This finding is comparable across cities, with Amman having a lower percentage (55 percent), Cairo having a higher percentage (59 percent), and Beirut having the highest (61 percent). Among women, only 28–36 percent of trips are made for work-related reasons.

In the three cities, personal and social activities (including social, medical, and care visits; accompanying someone else on their trip; and worship) are the main reasons women use public transport. Women are also more likely to use public transport for educational or shopping purposes (refer to figure 2.9). This finding is not surprising, because most working-age women in these cities are not economically active.

There are also a few variations by city. In Amman, a high percentage of women (29 percent) uses public transport for educational purposes as compared with Beirut and Cairo (15 percent each). In Beirut, the percentage of people using public transport for shopping is much lower than in other cities. Finally, in Cairo, the percentage of women using public transport for shopping as compared with men is very high.

How Much Time Do Men and Women Spend on Public Transport Trips?

While men and women spend a significant amount of time using public transport, on average, women tend to have slightly shorter trips than men. Table 2.1 shows the median length of trips by city and gender, while figure 2.10 presents their distribution by city.

Overall, trips tend to be shorter in Beirut than in Amman and Cairo. As compared with men, women tend to have slightly shorter trips in Beirut and Cairo (in Beirut, 45 minutes for men and 40 minutes for women; in Cairo, 60 minutes for men and 52 minutes for women). In Beirut and Cairo, women are also more likely than men to have trip durations of less than 30 minutes. However, in Amman, both men and women have a median length of a trip of 1 hour, and men are slightly more likely to have trips of less than 30 minutes.

On average, both men and women use several vehicles to complete their trip. In Amman, men and women use 1.8 and 1.9 vehicles, respectively, which is more than in Cairo (1.8 for men and 1.6 for women) and in Beirut (1.4 for men and 1.3 for women). Moreover, in all cities, some women were accompanied by another person on their trip

FIGURE 2.9

Purpose of Trips among Public Transport Users in Amman, Beirut, and Cairo

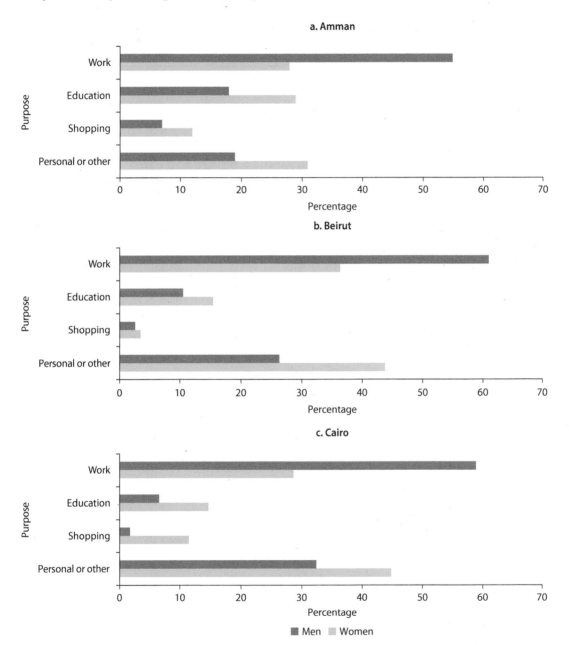

Source: Figure original to this publication using World Bank data: Public transport users surveys.
Note: These figures represent the share of all trips made by men and women for each purpose (based on reported trip origin and destination). In Amman and Beirut, the "Personal or other" category covers social, medical, and care visits; accompanying another traveler; worship; and other. In Cairo, the original survey only includes these four categories, with "Personal or other" being called "Personal."

TABLE 2.1

Median Time Spent on Trips Using Public Transport

City	Men	Women
Amman	60 minutes	60 minutes
Beirut	45 minutes	40 minutes
Cairo	60 minutes	52 minutes

Source: Table original to this publication using World Bank data: Public transport users surveys.
Note: Time may include stops made during the trips.

FIGURE 2.10

Length of Trips Using Public Transport in Amman, Beirut, and Cairo

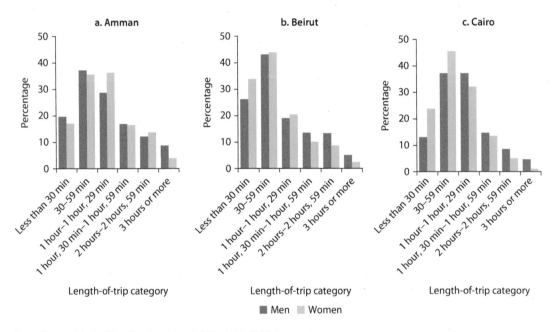

Source: Figure original to this publication using World Bank data: Public transport users surveys.
Note: Time may include stops made during the trips. min = minutes.

(24 percent, 27 percent, and 37 percent of women in Amman, Beirut, and Cairo, respectively), while fewer men were accompanied (14 percent, 16 percent, and 9 percent, in Amman, Beirut, and Cairo, respectively).[8]

How Much Money Do Men and Women Spend on Public Transport Trips?

In Beirut and Cairo, women tend to spend slightly less than men for public transport trips. In Amman, fares paid by men and women are similar. Table 2.2 shows the median fare of trips by city and gender, while figure 2.11 presents their distribution by city.

TABLE 2.2

Median Fare of Trips Using Public Transport

City	Men	Women
Amman, in JD	1	1
Beirut, in LP	30,000	25,000
Cairo, in EGP	6	5

Source: Table original to this publication using World Bank data: Public transport users surveys.
Note: These fares account for the entire trip made by the user, which may also include private vehicles and taxis. EGP = Egyptian pound; JD = Jordanian dinar; LP = Lebanese pound.

FIGURE 2.11

Distribution of Trip Fares Using Public Transport in Amman, Beirut, and Cairo, by Gender

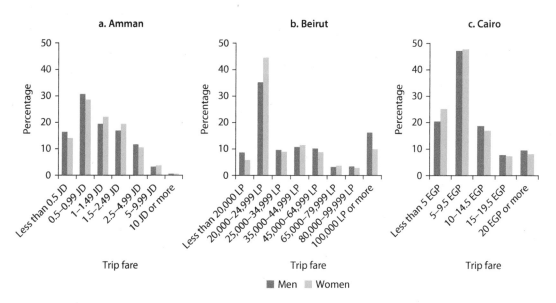

Source: Figure original to this publication World Bank data: Public transport users surveys.
Note: Note that these fares account for the entire trip made by user, which may also include private vehicles and taxis. JD = Jordanian dinar; LP = Lebanese pound; EGP = Egyptian pound.

The distribution of trip fares varies widely by city. In Amman, the price paid by public transport users varies more than in the other cities. The median fare is JD (Jordanian dinar) 1 for both men and women in Amman. In Beirut, most public transport users pay between LP (Lebanese pound) 20,000 and LP 24,999, and the median fare paid by women is slightly lower than that of men (LP 25,000 for women and LP 30,000 for men). In Cairo, most transport users pay between EGP (Egyptian pound) 5 and EGP 9.5, and the median fare for women

(EGP 5) is also slightly lower than that of men (EGP 6). However, even if women tend to pay slightly less than men for public transport trips, the money spent on transport may represent a higher share of their income or available budget.

What Public Transport Means Are Used in Each City?

Among public transport users, microbuses are the primary means of transport used by both men and women in each of the three cities. Figure 2.12 presents the various public transport means among users in each city.

In Amman, public transport users widely use all means (that is, buses or minibuses, microbuses, and services). Women are more likely than men to use buses or minibuses and are slightly less likely to use services.

In Beirut, microbuses are used much more than buses or minibuses. More than 80 percent of public transport users use microbuses. Women are less likely to use buses or minibuses than men.

In Cairo, about 60 percent of public transport users use microbuses, 40 percent use buses or minibuses, and about 10 percent use the metro trains. Men are more likely to use microbuses than women, but the share of men is similar to that of women for both buses or minibuses and the metro.

FIGURE 2.12

Means of Public Transport Used in Amman, Beirut, and Cairo, by Gender

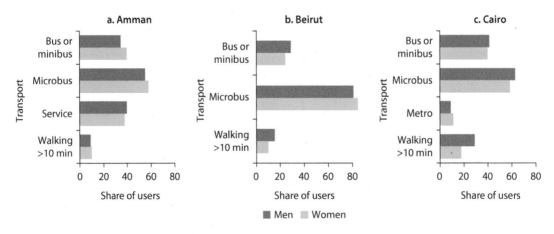

Source: Figure original to this publication using World Bank data: Public transport users surveys.
Note: These figures represent the shares of men and women among public transport users who use each means on their current trip. Public transport users may use multiple means.

For walking, significant differences exist among cities and between men and women. In Beirut and Cairo, more men than women walk 10 minutes or more on their public transport trip, while in Amman, more women do so than men. There are also differences in levels across cities. Only 10 percent of women walk 10 minutes or more in Amman and Beirut, while 18 percent do so in Cairo.

CHALLENGES AND AREAS OF IMPROVEMENT IDENTIFIED BY PUBLIC TRANSPORT USERS

This section illustrates the challenges men and women face in public transport and the areas for improvement.

What Are the Top Three Challenges for Women in Each City?

Women face different challenges in Amman, Beirut, and Cairo. Public transport users were asked to rate their means of transport on a scale from 1 to 5 along several dimensions. Figure 2.13 presents the three main challenges for women in each city.

In Amman, the main challenges relate to comfort (such as overcrowded vehicles) and the total length of trips (both waiting and trip times). Trip length and waiting time are also the main problems for women in Cairo, with cost being the third most salient challenge. However, in Beirut, trip

FIGURE 2.13

Top Three Challenges for Women Using Public Transport in Amman, Beirut, and Cairo

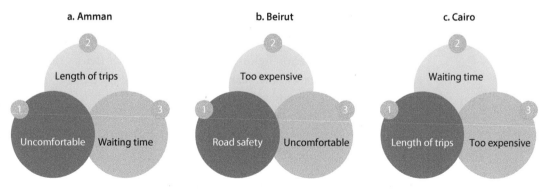

Source: Figure original to this publication using World Bank data: Public transport users surveys.

length does not appear in the top three challenges, as women are more concerned about road safety, trip cost, and lack of comfort.

The top three challenges are relatively similar among men and women. In Beirut, men identify the same top three challenges as women. In Cairo, men identify the same top two challenges; men ranked third the need to make transfers along the route rather than the cost of the trip. Finally, in Amman, men identify the same top issue as women but rank road safety as the second most important challenge and trip length as third.

Figure 2.14 presents the distribution of the satisfaction levels for each issue among men and women using public transport. This figure confirms the important differences by city, but men and women within each city tend to have similar answers.

What Are the Top Three Public Transport Issues That Women Would Like Improved?

Public transport users in Amman and Beirut were asked to identify their priority areas of improvement, both for the transport services and the auxiliary infrastructure at transport stops. The top three areas of improvement for women regarding transport services are somewhat different in Amman and Beirut (refer to figure 2.15). In Amman, women's top areas of improvement related to service coverage, service organization (both fixed stops and fixed scheduling), and then service frequency. In Beirut, the main areas of improvement identified by women relate to service cost, comfort, and coverage. The top three areas of improvement for men are the same as for women, except in Amman, where men prioritize fixed stops and scheduling over coverage.

For the top three areas of improvements in the auxiliary infrastructure at or near transport stops, women have similar answers in Amman and Beirut (refer to figure 2.15). In both cities, the main improvement area is the waiting areas at stops. In second place, women in Amman identify a need for bathroom facilities, whereas in Beirut, women identify station lighting. In both Amman and Beirut, the third improvement area was the quality of pavement and the general quality of access roads to stops.

The overall results from these questions are presented in figures 2.16 and 2.17.

FIGURE 2.14

Challenges among Public Transport Users in Amman, Beirut, and Cairo, by Gender

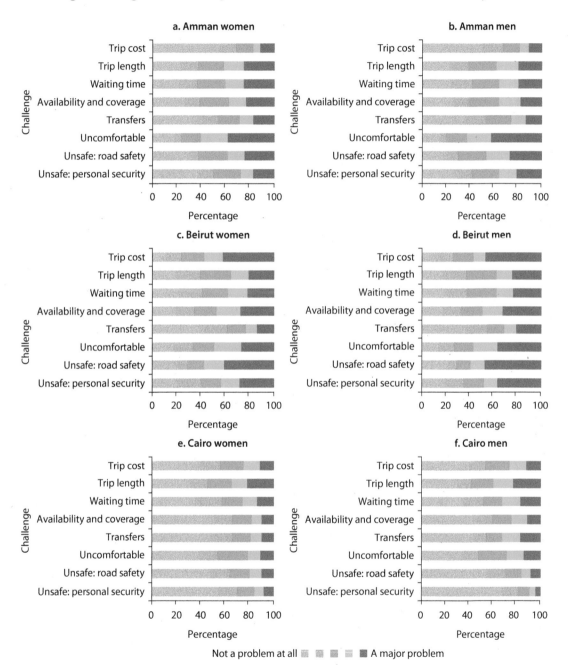

Source: Figure original to this publication using World Bank data: Public transport users surveys.

FIGURE 2.15

Top Three Areas for Improvements in Transport Services and Auxiliary Infrastructure in Amman, Beirut, and Cairo, as Identified by Women

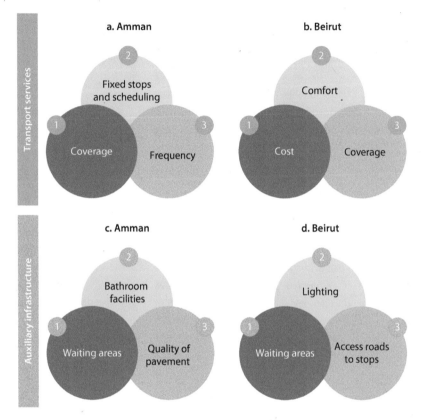

Source: Figure original to this publication using World Bank data: Public transport users surveys.

CONCLUSION

This chapter assesses the role of gender as a determinant of mobility choices and constraints. Three main conclusions emerge from the discussion.

First, women's and men's overall mobility patterns differ. Across Amman, Beirut, and Cairo, men are more mobile, rely more on private vehicles, and are more likely to have driver's licenses. In contrast, women in all three cities are likely to be more dependent on others (male household members driving them, taxis, or the equivalent) and on public transport to meet their mobility needs.

Second, important gender- and city-based variations exist in the use of public transport. Private vehicles are the main mode of transport in

FIGURE 2.16

Top Improvements Identified for Public Transport Services in Amman and Beirut, by Gender

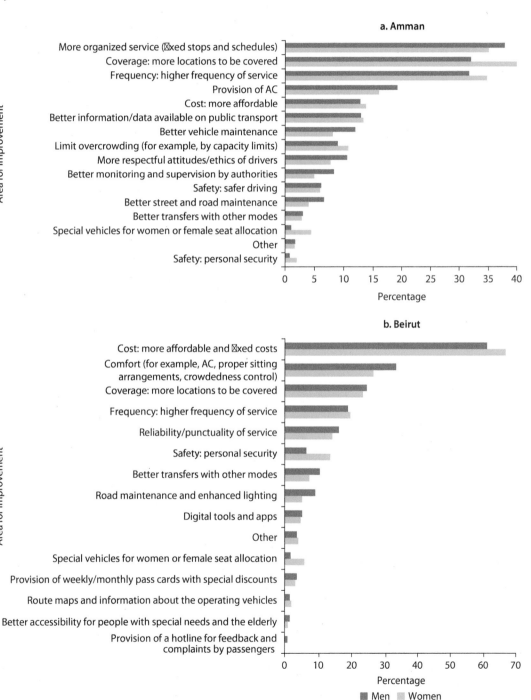

Source: Figure original to this publication using World Bank data: Public transport users surveys.
Note: Respondents were asked to identify the top two areas that would improve public transport. AC = air conditioning.

FIGURE 2.17

Top Improvements Identified for Auxiliary Infrastructure in and Near Transport Stops in Amman and Beirut, by Gender

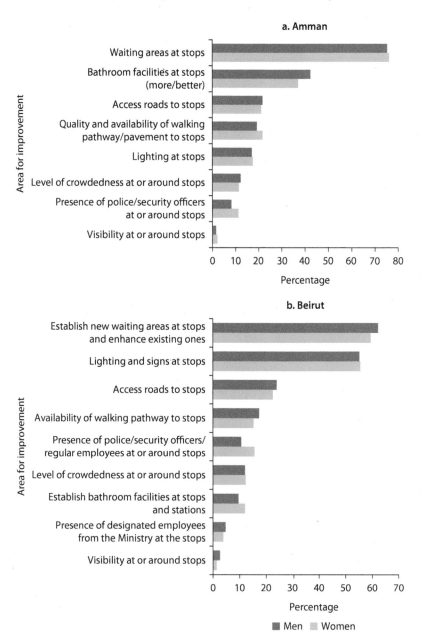

Source: Figure original to this publication using World Bank data: Public transport users surveys.
Note: Respondents were asked to identify the top two aspects of the access to or area surrounding public transport stops that could be improved.

Amman and Beirut for both women and men, whereas public transport is the primary choice for both women and men in Cairo. Regardless, in all three cities, men are more likely than women to use public transport daily.

Among public transport users, microbuses are the primary means of public transport for men and women in each city. Completing a trip by public transport is time-consuming, because it requires almost 1 hour, on average, in Amman and Cairo and 45 minutes in Beirut, as well as multiple vehicles. The main purpose of public transport use differs between men and women. In the three cities, work is the main reason for using public transport among men, whereas personal and other activities (including social, medical, and care visits; accompanying someone else on their trip; and worship) are the main reasons women use public transport.

Third, when using public transport, women face different barriers in each city, but the challenges faced by men and women within each city are relatively similar. This finding affirms that fundamental deficiencies in the public transport system affect both men and women. In Amman, the three main challenges for women using public transport are uncomfortable riding environments, long trip times, and long wait times. In Beirut, the three main challenges are road safety concerns, the cost or affordability of public transport, and uncomfortable riding environments. In Cairo, the three main challenges are long trip times, long wait times, and the cost or affordability of using public transport.

NOTES

1. Included are the purpose of the trips, as well as their length, cost, and mode choices.
2. Some of the CTA services are operated by private companies under a concession to the CTA.
3. Included are companies with codes AGY, GRN, and MSR.
4. In the rest of the report, to have comparability across cities, *coasters* in Amman are referred to as *microbuses*.
5. In the rest of the report, to have comparability across cities, *minivans* in Beirut are referred to as *microbuses*.
6. Details relating to services and taxis can be found in the forthcoming Lebanon Public Transport Diagnostic.
7. For mass transit, people are willing to walk farther and for longer, as this mode tends to travel at higher speeds.
8. In Amman and Beirut, women were accompanied by children in 6 percent and 5 percent, respectively, of all trips. These figures are 1 percent and 2 percent, respectively, among men. Data on the identity of the accompanying persons is not available for Cairo.

REFERENCES

Elias, W., J. Benjamin, and Y. Shiftan. 2015. "Gender Differences in Activity and Travel Behavior in the Arab World." *Transport Policy* 44: 19–27. doi:10.1016/j .tranpol.2015.07.001.

Morad, M. A. Ardila Gomez, H. A. A. Al-Aghbari, M. M. Alam, Y. Li, N. Daito, S. Nobuhiko, G. Samaha, O. E. Diaz, M. J. Sala Pelufo, and S. A. A. O. Aloul. 2022. *Jordan Public Transport Diagnostic and Recommendations (English)*. World Bank, Washington, DC. https://documents1.worldbank.org/curated/en /099825106052213281/pdf/P17389502814af03b0a85e0a27bbbbaa260.pdf.

Tennøy, A., M. Knapskog, and F. Wolday. 2022. "Walking Distances to Public Transport in Smaller and Larger Norwegian Cities." *Transportation Research Part D: Transport and Environment* 103: 103169. https://doi.org/10.1016/j .trd.2022.103169.

van Soest, D., M. R. Tight, and C. D. Rogers. 2020. "Exploring the Distances People Walk to Access Public Transport." *Transport Reviews* 40 (2): 160–182. https://doi.org/10.1080/01441647.2019.1575491.

World Bank. 2022. "Green Transition of Transport in Egypt: Updates from Greater Cairo Mobility Assessment and Public Transport Improvement Study (MAPTIS)." Presentation. World Bank, Washington, DC. https://events .wbgkggtf.org/sites/kggtf_events/files/session/KGID_Greater%20Cairo%20 MAPTIS%20Overview.pdf.

CHAPTER 3

Mobility, Gender, and Access to Economic Opportunities

BACKGROUND

Many people from lower- and middle-income families rely on the public transport system as a lifeline to reach economic opportunities. In Amman, Beirut, and Cairo, many public transport users face high costs of commuting, long commuting distances and times, long wait times, uncomfortable commuting conditions, and unsafe roads. In turn, these deficiencies can inhibit commuters' use of the public transport system, leading to unmet mobility needs. This situation hints at historically insufficient investments in public transport, the prioritization of cars over mass transit and other shared modes of transport, and a lack of policies that promote mass transit and shared transport over private modes. Because low- and middle-income workers are especially dependent on public transport, better access to public transport can help reduce inequality by improving labor market outcomes.

Do deficiencies in the public transport system inhibit women from being economically productive members of society? What facets of the public transport system matter for women? Do some aspects matter more than others? How much more could women contribute to the economic output if public transport constraints were alleviated? This chapter discusses these questions in the context of three urban areas: Amman in Jordan; Beirut in Lebanon, and Cairo in the Arab Republic of Egypt.

The chapter first reviews the obstacles encountered by individuals, which includes an examination of the mobility choices and barriers faced by workers commuting as well as the barriers faced by those who are not currently employed. Then, the chapter provides an analysis of the causal effects of the transport systems and their associated barriers to women's economic activity. Two measures of economic activity are used in the analysis:

- The *labor force participation (LFP) rate*, which measures the share of the working-age population working or actively seeking employment, and

- The *employment rate*, which measures the share of the working-age population that is gainfully employed in a job or is self-employed.

WHY MOBILITY MATTERS FOR THE LABOR MARKET

While enhancing transport connectivity—including better access to public transport and higher job accessibility—has been associated with improved employment probabilities for both men and women (Bastiaanssen, Johnson, and Lucas 2020), women's economic activity tends to be more sensitive to deficiencies in the transport system. Evidence from developed and developing countries demonstrates how gender inequities in transport access create worse employment outcomes for women than for men, sometimes even within the same household (Alam et al. 2022).

In formal and informal employment, women tend to work closer to home, often due to child-rearing or household responsibilities. However, formally employed individuals, irrespective of gender, tend to travel longer distances by public transport or by car. Affordability constraints, mainly due to low incomes earned by women, significantly affect women's use of transport.[1] For some, the cost of travel and time taken in commuting may be so prohibitive that they prefer to remain in long-term unemployment rather than pursue well-paying employment options in farther-away locations within the city. For others, security concerns in public spaces (including public transport) and the lack of a comfortable environment when using public transport systems may be critical inhibitors. Still for others, the walking distance to the closest public transport stop and the time spent waiting for the next available transport vehicle might inhibit the desire to seek gainful employment.

Improving the availability, accessibility, affordability, acceptability, and safety and security of public transport can transform the economic lives of both women and men and their families. The potential economic gains from improving public transport systems can be wide-ranging. Improving the public transport system means that more women can participate in the labor market, and those already participating can access a broader range of jobs, increasing the chances of finding employment that is a better match for their skills. These improvements can also connect small business owners (who often are self-employed) to potential suppliers, thus enabling access to better-quality or lower-cost inputs, and to potential customers, thus enhancing the demand for their businesses. Therefore, improving public transport connectivity can increase productivity and employment, leading to higher economic output.

MOBILITY PATTERNS OF PEOPLE WHO CURRENTLY WORK

How do workers commute from home to work and back? Which modes are used in each city? Do women and men use the same modes? This section presents the travel patterns of workers on their commutes.

Does a Sizeable Share of People Work from Home?

Most workers do not work from home. This fact is particularly true of men; in all three cities, between 97 percent and 98 percent of working men work outside the home. Most working women also work outside the home, but this trend is more prominent in Beirut (96 percent) and Amman (89 percent) than in Cairo (76 percent).

Which Mode of Transport Do Workers Use for Commuting?

Important differences exist in the commuting patterns of workers both within and between cities. In Amman and Beirut, private vehicles constitute the main mode of transport for commuters, while in Cairo, public transport is the main mode. Only a small share of people who commute to work use public transport as their main mode in Amman and Beirut (around 10 percent of both women and men), whereas almost half the commuters use public transport in Cairo (47 percent of women and 44 percent of men) (refer to figure 3.1). This finding is in line with the overall mobility patterns of the population (for not only work-related trips) as presented in figure 2.2.

A standout trend in Amman is the reliance on private buses provided by employers, which account for 10 percent of the trips for women and 3 percent for men. In Beirut, private buses are almost negligible; in Cairo, their share of use is 4 percent for women and 3 percent for men.

FIGURE 3.1

Dominant Mode of Transport for Commuting from Home to Work in Amman, Beirut, and Cairo, by Gender

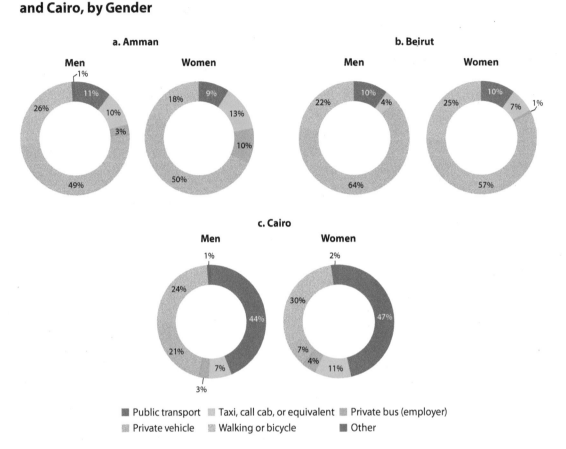

Source: Figure original to this publication using World Bank data: Household surveys.
Note: In Amman, the services are included in the category "Taxi, call cab, or equivalent."

How Do Men's and Women's Transport Choices Vary by City?

The share of women using public transport as compared to men is lower in Amman, is similar in Beirut, and is higher in Cairo. The share of women relying on private vehicles is like that of men in Amman, but in Beirut and Cairo, fewer women than men rely on private vehicles. However, the share of women using a taxi or equivalent as their main commuting mode is higher than that of men in each of the three cities (7 percent of women in Beirut, 11 percent in Cairo, and 13 percent in Amman; refer to figure 3.1).

Finally, a sizable share of people commute in all three cities by only walking (bicycles are rarely used). This share is larger for women than men in both Beirut and Cairo, while there are fewer women than men who only walk in Amman.

Which Types of Public Transport Are Most Widely Used for Commuting in Each City?

The main means of public transport for commuters is the same for men and women within each of the three cities: microbus in Amman and Cairo and bus or minibus in Beirut. In Cairo, the metro train is the second-most-used means of public transport; it is used more frequently than buses and minibuses (refer to figure 3.2).

THE LATENT DESIRE TO BE GAINFULLY EMPLOYED

Is there a latent demand for economic opportunities? What factors are constraining men and women from being gainfully employed? Is the lack of suitable transport options a key barrier that keeps women from exercising their right to work? This section identifies the barriers to gainful employment, as reported by individuals.

FIGURE 3.2

Dominant Means of Public Transport for Commuting from Home to Work in Amman, Beirut, and Cairo, by Gender

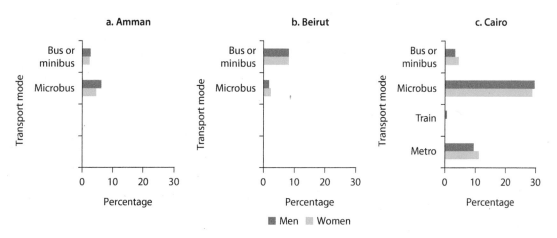

Source: Figure original to this publication using World Bank data: Household surveys.

Labor Force Participation

This section presents the gaps between men and women in LFP in each country and investigates whether transport is a binding constraint to work.

Do Gaps Exist in LFP between Men and Women in Each Country?

A large gap exists between male and female LFP rates in all three countries. The share of female-to-male LFP rate is the lowest in Egypt at 22 percent, followed closely by Jordan at 24 percent and Lebanon at 43 percent.[2]

Is Transport a Binding Constraint for People Who Are Not Currently Working?

In each city, people who are currently not working were asked if they aspire to be economically active. Most non-working women say they would be willing to accept a job if it were available (refer to figure 3.3). There is a high work latency among women in these three cities.

Commuting as a Barrier to Work

The answers to the following questions can help determine if and how commuting is a barrier to work.

Is Commuting a Barrier to Work?

In Amman and Beirut, most non-working women and men see commuting as a barrier to work. In Cairo, twice as many women as men consider

FIGURE 3.3

Share of Non-Working Women Who Say They Would Be Willing to Accept a Job If It Were Available in Amman, Beirut, and Cairo

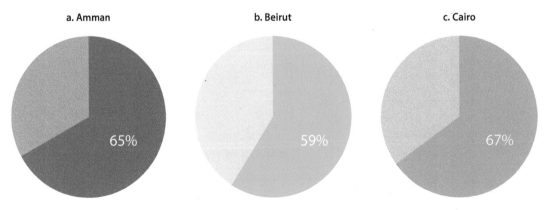

a. Amman: 65% b. Beirut: 59% c. Cairo: 67%

Source: Figure original to this publication using World Bank data: Household surveys.

commuting an obstacle to employment. There are important differences by city in the perception of commuting being a barrier to work for those who are not currently working (refer to figure 3.4).

Amman has the strongest perception of commuting being an obstacle to employment, with more than 60 percent of non-working men and women citing it as a barrier. Beirut showed similar results but with slightly lower shares, at about 53 percent. In contrast, significant differences exist between the perception of women and men in Cairo, as nearly 50 percent of women view commuting as a barrier to work, while only 26 percent of men do so.

Why Is Commuting a Barrier to Work?

Do transport-related barriers (for example, trip length) or non-transport reasons (such as family preferences) pose a barrier to men and women working? Figure 3.5 presents the reasons given by non-working individuals who consider commuting a barrier to work.

Men mainly cite transport-related reasons for commuting as being a barrier to work, while women, especially in Cairo, report non-transport reasons more frequently. More than 97 percent of men in each of the three cities report only transport reasons, while 86 percent of women in Amman and 84 percent of women in Beirut do so (refer to figure 3.5). In Cairo, only 45 percent of women report transport-related reasons exclusively, while 22 percent report exclusively non-transport reasons, and the remaining 33 percent report both types of issues. In Amman and Beirut, a sizable share of women reports that a combination of transport and non–transport-related reasons pose a

FIGURE 3.4

Percentage of Non-Working People Who Perceive That Commuting Is a Barrier to Work in Amman, Beirut, and Cairo, by Gender

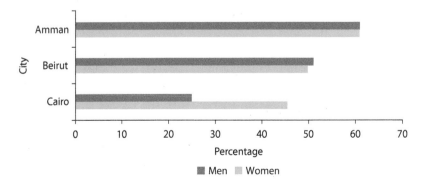

Source: Figure original to this publication using World Bank data: Household surveys.

FIGURE 3.5

Reasons Cited by Non-Working People Who Consider Commuting as a Barrier to Work in Amman, Beirut, and Cairo, by Gender

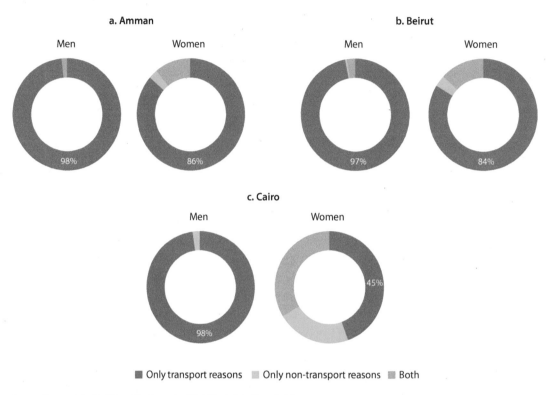

Source: Figure original to this publication using World Bank data: Household surveys.

barrier for them. This finding suggests that, while commuting barriers for men are strongly linked to the transport system, women also face important additional external barriers. These additional external barriers demonstrate that scarcity of available time can be a significant challenge for women's labor force participation (refer to box 3.1).

Which Transport Constraints Are the Most Relevant for Men and Women?

Among transport barriers to commuting, the cost of the trips is the main barrier for men and women in Amman and Beirut. In Cairo, the length of the trips for both is the main barrier, with the cost of trips second. However, the relative importance of this financial constraint for women and men differs by city.

In Amman, the cost of trips is a larger concern for women, while in Cairo, it is more of an issue for men. In Beirut, the cost of trips is equally important for women and men, accounting for 50 percent of the total

BOX 3.1

Women's Time Poverty

For women, particularly for those with children, the scarcity of available time can be a significant challenge. This scarcity is known as *time poverty*, which arises from women's disproportionate burden from unpaid care activities and domestic work, including taking care of children, household maintenance, and other domestic tasks. Time poverty prevents women from accessing services and activities related to physical and mental health, education, professional development, and paid work. Overall, this issue points to the many distinct challenges and constraints in women's final decision to seek employment (Alam et al. 2022; United Nations 2019).

In Egypt, women ages 15–64 spend, on average, 24 hours per week on unpaid direct and indirect care work,[a] whereas men spend, on average, only 2 hours per week on similar tasks. Importantly, even when employed, women spend a significant share of their time on care work. While unemployed women spend 24 hours per week on care work, employed women spend 25 hours per week, which is added to their 38 average hours of paid work. However, both non-employed and employed men spend only 2 hours per week on care work (Selwaness and Helmy 2020).[b]

In Jordan, the results are similar to those of Egypt. Women ages 15–64 spend, on average, 19 hours per week on unpaid direct and indirect care as compared with only 1 hour for men. These weekly hours apply both to non-employed women (19 hours of care work per week) and employed women (20 weekly hours of care work on top of the 37 hours of paid work), while both non-employed and employed men only spend 1 hour on similar tasks (Alhawarin et al. 2020).[c] A more recent survey of time use among married couples with children reveals that mothers within a household spend, on average, 5 hours and 45 minutes more than their husband per weekday on direct and indirect care work (Redaelli et al. 2023).[d]

In Lebanon, while a strict comparison with the data of Jordan and Egypt is not available for total hours of unpaid direct and indirect care work per week among women and men in the overall population, the recent survey by Redaelli et al. (2023) shows that women bear a much larger burden of unpaid care work as compared to men. Among married couples with children, mothers spend at least 7 more hours per weekday of unpaid direct and indirect care work than fathers within the same household.[e]

a. Direct care work includes childcare, elderly care, and sick or disabled care. Indirect care includes all unpaid domestic chores.
b. Data are from 2012.
c. Data are from 2016.
d. Data are from 2021, but questions on care activities concern activities before the COVID-19 pandemic.
e. Data are from 2021, but questions on care activities concern activities before the COVID-19 pandemic.

issues (refer to figure 3.6). In Cairo, the length of the commuting trips is the main problem facing men and women, while in Amman, it is the second-most-reported issue. In both instances, this issue is more salient for men than women. In Beirut, however, trip length is not a main barrier for commuting to work.

Personal security and comfort are more salient barriers for women than men. For women, personal security is a salient barrier in Beirut and Cairo, where it represents 13 percent and 12 percent of the total issues, respectively (in Beirut, it is the second-most-important issue for women). In comparison, in Amman, personal security represents only 5 percent of issues among women and is the least frequently cited reason for commuting being a barrier to work. For men in Amman and Cairo, personal security is almost never chosen; in Beirut, 9 percent of men report personal security to be a barrier. Comfort is particularly important for women in Cairo, who cite it three times more frequently than men as a barrier.

However, public transport frequency is a relatively more important barrier among men than women in each of the three cities. Public transport coverage (close to residential locations or workplaces) has the same relative weight for both men and women.

FIGURE 3.6

Relative Importance of Transport-Related Barriers to Commuting for Work in Amman, Beirut, and Cairo, by Gender

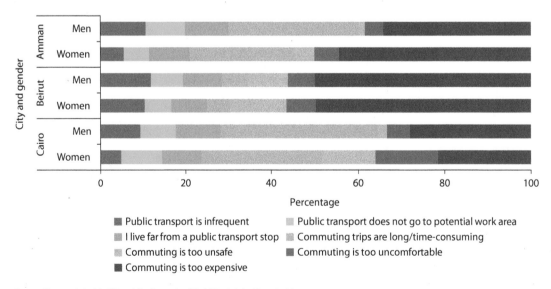

Source: Figure original to this publication using World Bank data: Household surveys.
Note: The figure shows the relative importance of each issue among all respondents who cited at least one transport barrier to commuting as being a barrier to work.

FIGURE 3.7

Relative Importance of Non–Transport-Related Barriers to Women Commuting for Work in Amman, Beirut, and Cairo

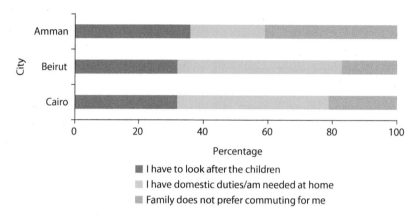

Source: Figure original to this publication using World Bank data: Household surveys.
Note: The figure shows the relative importance of each issue among all women who cited at least one non-transport barrier to commuting as being a barrier to work.

Which Non-Transport Constraints Are the Most Important Barriers?

Family preference against women commuting is the main non-transport barrier to commuting in Amman, while domestic duties are the main constraint in Beirut and Cairo (refer to figure 3.7).

SPATIAL MEASURES OF MOBILITY BY PUBLIC AND ACTIVE MEANS OF TRANSPORT

The previous section relied on self-reported data to shed light on the "latent desire" to be economically active and the barriers to commuting for work. While this method has many advantages, it also has several shortcomings, such as exaggerated or understated responses, responders' perceived embarrassment at revealing the actual reason behind a particular choice, responders' underreporting specific types of constraints (for example, concerns for personal safety) due to social taboos, and systematic unreliability in measurement in specific types of questions.[3]

These issues are averted by first constructing objective (spatially granular) measures of three important facets of the public transport system for all three cities, as discussed in this section:

- The (spatial) accessibility of jobs through public transport and walking,

- The availability of public transport close to residential locations, and

- The safety of built environments to measure the level of security around public transport stops.

Next, men's and women's employment choices are analyzed in relation to the constructed measures of public transport quality. While the affordability of public transport is an important dimension that should be included, this was not possible due to data limitations. The rest of the section presents the methodology used to construct the spatial measures or indicators and the results for each city.[4]

Accessibility of Jobs Using Public Transport in Amman, Beirut, and Cairo

The first spatial measure of mobility focuses on the accessibility of jobs using public transport and walking. Accessibility is a critical indicator of women's mobility and access to economic empowerment, as it directly affects their ability to access job opportunities. Furthermore, at the city level, spatial accessibility to economic opportunities is a key enabler of efficient labor markets, leading to agglomeration economies, economic development, and social inclusion.

Three data sources were used to measure the accessibility of jobs throughout each city spatially. The first data source used was the public transport network, including the frequencies of departure and speeds by which the public transport vehicles travel on the mapped routes (refer to chapter 2, the "Public Transport Networks and Their Use" section for details and maps about these data). These data were combined with a layer of the street composition for each city—street grid data are taken from OpenStreetMap.[5] Finally, the developed public transport and road network map were combined with the relative density of employment across each metropolitan area, which was estimated using the distribution of employment in each city,[6] and population density. For each location, this accessibility measure provides an estimate of the total jobs in the city that are accessible within 60 minutes of travel time using only public transport and walking.[7] This measure is closely linked to a key challenge and area of improvement identified by public transport users in Amman, Beirut, and Cairo (refer to figures 2.14 and 2.16). The length of trip was in the top three challenges identified in both Amman and Cairo.

Map 3.1 presents the maps of the accessibility of jobs through public transport in Amman, Beirut, and Cairo. These maps show the spatial distribution of the share of total jobs accessible through public transport throughout each city and illustrate that the accessibility of jobs is uneven within cities.

MAP 3.1

Accessibility of Public Transport in Amman, Beirut, and Cairo

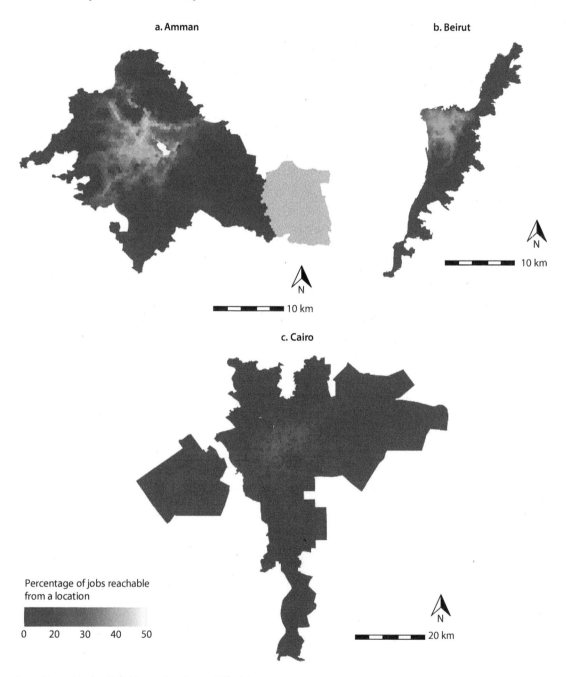

a. Amman

b. Beirut

c. Cairo

Percentage of jobs reachable
from a location

0   20   30   40   50

Source: Maps original to this publication based on World Bank data: Transit network mapping; OpenStreetMap; WorldPop; and Barzin et al.
2022.

On average, Amman, Beirut, and Cairo have low accessibility levels. Figure 3.8 further presents the average accessibility levels in each city. People in Amman can reach 18 percent of the total jobs in under 60 minutes using public transport and walking; in Beirut, the figure is 30 percent, and in Cairo, which is a larger city,[8] 13 percent.[9] These low accessibility levels point to the need for several actions, including prioritizing public transport through integrated corridor management or the creation of or improvements to mass transit like bus rapid transit or metro trains; improving existing land regulations to foster dense, diverse, and well-designed urban development; and enhancing the walkability of the cities by improving sidewalks and walkways and developing pedestrian-first policies.

The accessibility of destinations depends on the time of departure from home. The accessibility levels for individuals depend on whether jobs are accessible in less than a fixed time (60 minutes in the analysis). However, depending on the departure time from home, a trip to the same location may take a different amount of time when a transport service runs every 5 minutes than when it runs every 15 minutes. For situations of relatively high frequency or for transport service that is not scheduled, people often wait at the station for the next available transport option. In practice, however, the length of this wait will affect the average trip time, and the same job might be inaccessible depending on the departure time.

To account for this issue, the accessibility analysis was run multiple times over the course of the 8:00 am–9:00 am time window, and a destination was considered reachable if it could be reached at least 50 percent of the time. While the main analysis fixes the total travel time at 60 minutes and the minimum reachability threshold at 50 percent,

FIGURE 3.8

Average Accessibility Levels in Amman, Beirut, and Cairo

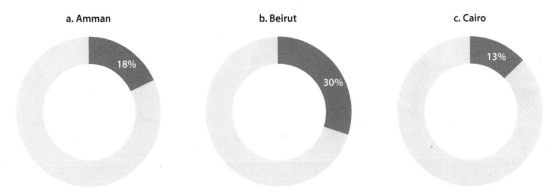

Source: Figure original to this publication based on World Bank data: Transit network mapping; OpenStreetMap; WorldPop; and Barzin et al. 2022.
Note: The estimation uses population-weighted averages. A travel time of 60 minutes and a minimum reachability threshold of 50 percent were used.

results for a threshold of 45 minutes as well as minimum reachability levels of 10 percent and 90 percent are also reported. The sensitivity of the results to these different parameters is presented in table 3.1. This analysis confirms that the average accessibility levels within each city are higher for 60 minutes than for 45 minutes and that they decrease if higher minimum reachability levels are imposed.

Besides examining the average accessibility levels within each city, it is interesting to determine how equal or unequal their distribution is. The equality of access is calculated by generating a Lorenz curve and Gini coefficients for the different thresholds and minimum reachability levels. The results for the Gini coefficients are presented in table 3.2. Higher Gini coefficients represent a more unequal distribution of accessibility to job opportunities across the population. For all three cities, the distribution of access is highly unequal.

Shorter and more reliable trips to employment sites are even more unequally distributed than longer and unreliable trips. When comparing the cities, Beirut has higher accessibility levels, on average, and lower inequality levels in access. However, while Amman has a higher average accessibility than Cairo, it also has higher inequality levels. The Lorenz curves are presented in figure 3.9.

TABLE 3.1

Average Accessibility Levels for Different Parameters

City	Time	Low minimum reachability threshold (10%)	Medium minimum reachability threshold (50%)	High minimum reachability threshold (90%)
Amman	60 minutes	24.8	**18.3**	13.2
	45 minutes	12.1	7.7	4.8
Beirut	60 minutes	34.4	**29.8**	24.7
	45 minutes	20.3	15.6	11.8
Cairo	60 minutes	15.3	**12.6**	10.4
	45 minutes	6.7	5.1	3.8

Source: Table original to this publication based on World Bank data: Transit network mapping; OpenStreetMap; WorldPop; and Barzin et al. 2022.
Note: **Bold** cells are the main parameters used in the analysis.

TABLE 3.2

Gini Index of Accessibility Levels for Different Parameters

City	Time	Low minimum reachability threshold (10%)	Medium minimum reachability threshold (50%)	High minimum reachability threshold (90%)
Amman	60 minutes	0.57	**0.63**	0.67
	45 minutes	0.66	0.70	0.72
Beirut	60 minutes	0.41	**0.44**	0.47
	45 minutes	0.51	0.53	0.55
Cairo	60 minutes	0.50	**0.52**	0.53
	45 minutes	0.56	0.58	0.59

Source: Table original to this publication based on World Bank data: Transit network mapping; OpenStreetMap; WorldPop; and Barzin et al. 2022.
Note: **Bold** cells are the main parameters used in the analysis.

FIGURE 3.9

Lorenz Curves of Accessibility Levels for Different Parameters of Public Transport in Amman, Beirut, and Cairo

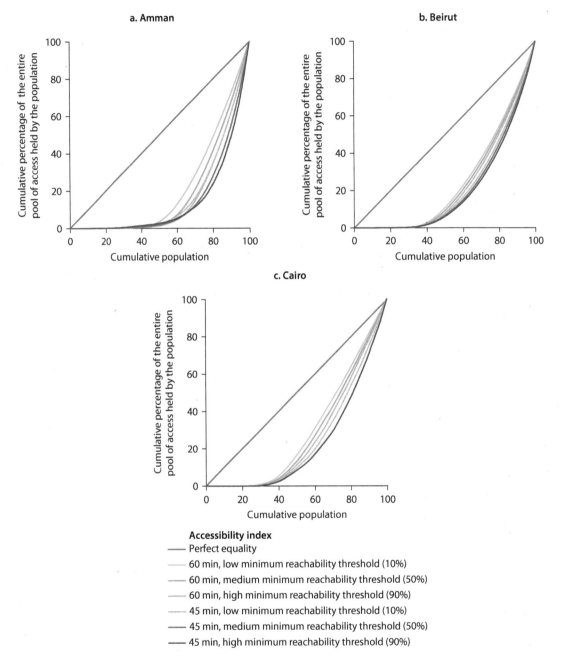

Source: Figure original to this publication based on World Bank data: Transit network mapping; OpenStreetMap; WorldPop; and Barzin et al. 2022.

In all three cities, workers who live in areas with better accessibility are less likely to commute to work using private vehicles and are more likely to use public transport and to walk. Figure 3.10 presents the commuters' choice of mode for every percentile of accessibility level in each city and illustrates how the mode share changes from the lowest level (percentile 0) of accessibility in the city to the highest (percentile 100). In the three cities, the prevalence of private vehicles for commuters visibly decreases with an increase in accessibility. However, walking and public transport become more widely used for commuting as the accessibility of jobs increases.

In Amman, the decrease in private vehicles is mainly offset by a large increase in walking and shared transport (which, in Amman, also include services that are a part of the route-based public transport network). In Beirut, the decrease in using private vehicles when accessibility rises is mainly offset by walking to work. Public transport also increases from an average of 7 percent of commuters in the lowest quintile of accessibility to an average of 12 percent in the highest quintile. Finally, in Cairo, public

FIGURE 3.10

Commuter's Mode Choice and Accessibility Levels in Amman, Beirut, and Cairo, by Transport Type

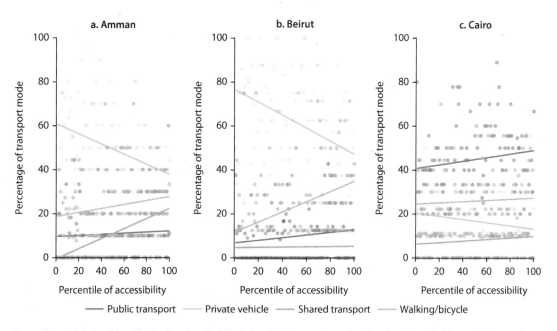

Source: Figure original to this publication based on World Bank data: Transit network mapping; OpenStreetMap; WorldPop; and Barzin et al. 2022.
Note: The dominant mode is defined as the motorized mode on which the respondent spends most of their usual work commute and as walking or using a bicycle, if no other motorized mode is used. Shared transport includes taxi and equivalent modes. In Amman, shared transport also includes services.

transport is the main mode of transport for all levels of accessibility, but it increases with accessibility while the use of private modes decreases.

Public Transport Availability in Amman, Beirut, and Cairo

Availability, which is the second spatial measure of mobility, relates to the proximity of public transport to residential locations. In practice, this measure is based on the proximity to public transport stops, factoring in the frequency of service. This indicator is used to assess the density of service within the immediate reach of the household but without considering the destinations of the public transport. This measure complements the measure of accessibility, which encompasses the full journey to employment opportunities through public transport.

The availability of public transport close to residential locations (both the geographic proximity of public transport stops and the frequency of service) is an important consideration for women when using public transport. This issue is also highlighted in the challenges and areas of improvement identified by public transport users in Amman, Beirut, and Cairo (refer to figures 2.14 and 2.16). Wait time at public transport stops was a top three challenge identified in both Amman and Cairo.

Two sources of data were used to measure the availability throughout each city spatially. Like the measure of accessibility, measuring availability also relies on transit network data and street grid data from OpenStreetMap.[10] For each location, the number of public transport "runs" are computed, which is the number of vehicle departures at all stops available within a 10-minute walking time over the course of an hour.[11] The number of runs is normalized to create an index between 0 and 100 percent.[12] A value of 100 percent means that public transport is highly available within a 10-minute walking distance of a household. In contrast, a value of 0 means that no public transport is available within a 10-minute walking distance of a household.

Map 3.2 presents the maps of the availability of public transport in Amman, Beirut, and Cairo. These maps show the spatial distribution of the availability of public transport throughout each city, illustrating that the availability of public transport is, on average, higher in the central areas of each metropolitan region and along the public transport routes.

An average index of availability is also computed for each city. Because some areas with low-density population might have low availability, the averages of availability are weighted by population density (refer to figure 3.11). These averages show that people living in Beirut have a higher availability of public transport close to residential locations than those in Cairo and in Amman, which has the lowest availability among the three cities.

MAP 3.2

Availability of Public Transport in Amman, Beirut, and Cairo

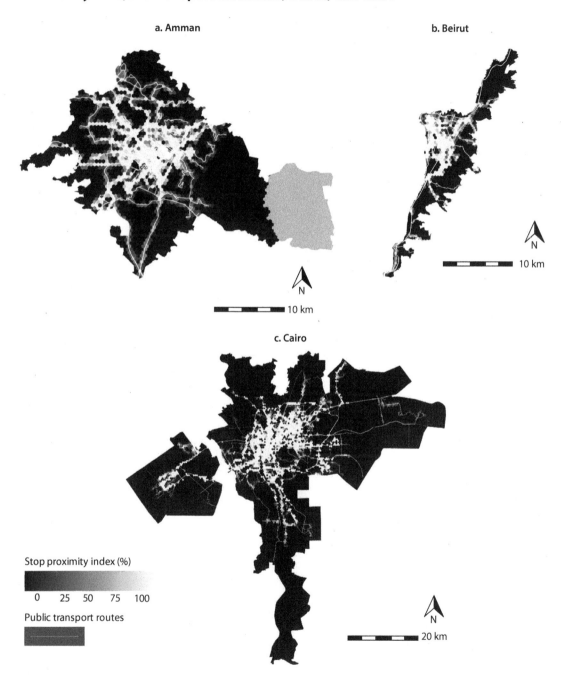

Source: Maps original to this publication based on World Bank data: Transit network mapping and OpenStreetMap.

FIGURE 3.11

Average Availability Levels in Amman, Beirut, and Cairo

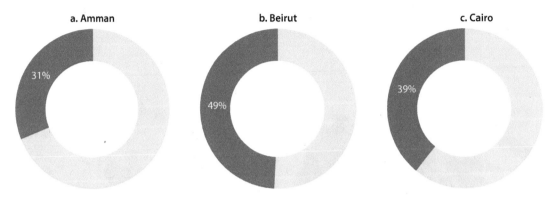

Source: Figure original to this publication based on World Bank data: Transit network mapping; OpenStreetMap; and WorldPop.
Note: Population-weighted averages were used for the estimation.

Public Transport Safety in Amman, Beirut, and Cairo

Women's experience of public transport also differs from that of men for issues related to harassment and personal security, which is why the third spatial measure is the safety of public transport. This measure examines the level of personal security at or near public transport stops. Security includes both sexual harassment and the incidence of crimes.

Safety at or near public transport stops is a crucial aspect of personal security for women. For instance, in Jordan, 64 percent of women have been harassed for being a woman while using public transport.

Most occurrences of harassment happen in the street, either while walking (24 percent) or while waiting for transport (18 percent), at a bus station (16 percent), or at a transport stop (15 percent). In comparison, harassment on public transport is slightly lower and depends on the means of transport (from 6 percent in services to 14 percent on buses) (Aloul, Naffa, and Mansour 2018).

Safety is measured using the built environment audits conducted in each city. In each metropolitan area, 50 public transport stops were audited.[13] Each public transport stop is assessed based on seven parameters (refer to figure 3.12) to objectively and comprehensively assess various dimensions associated with the perception of safety at or near public transport stops. These built environment audits first allow the provision of the disaggregated results for each parameter to demonstrate the relative importance of each aspect of personal security in Amman, Beirut, and Cairo, and second, to construct a spatial measure of safety to understand spatial heterogeneities within each city.

Important differences exist in the various aspects of the built environment in Amman, Beirut, and Cairo. Figure 3.13 presents the results of

FIGURE 3.12

Parameters Used to Assess Safety at Public Transport Stops

Source: Figure created using method from Safetipin.
Note: Each parameter is defined as follows: (1) *Light:* The availability of lighting infrastructure, on a scale from none to bright; (2) *Walking path:* The presence of sidewalks, from none to good; (3) *Openness:* The ability to see and move in all directions, from not open to completely open; (4) *Visibility:* The presence of vendors, shops, building entrances, windows, and balconies from where one can be seen, from no eyes (out of sight of others) to highly visible; (5) *Security:* The presence of police or security guards, from none to high; (6) *People:* The number of people around the respondent, from deserted to crowded; and (7) *Gender usage:* The presence of women near the respondent, from none to the majority being women.

the built environment audits for each city. In Amman, the majority of the surveyed public transport stops lack the presence of guards or police and have a low number of women present. However, on average, public transport stops have a substantial level of openness and visibility and a sufficient number of people present. More problems exist in Beirut than in the two other cities. The majority of public transport stops lack good lighting at night.[14] There is also a low presence of guards or police (but comparable with the other cities), a low presence of people overall, and a low presence of women at public transport stops. All these factors can impose strong barriers to the use of public transport by women.

There are fewer major concerns in Cairo than in Beirut, but most public transport stops present at least some problems in all aspects except for the sufficient number of people present. In particular, as compared with the other cities, only a minority of surveyed stops have good pavement quality and good levels of openness and visibility.

The behavior of other public transport users and bystanders is a key determinant of perceived and realized levels of safety. This behavior

FIGURE 3.13

Safety at Public Transport Stops: Results from the Built Environment Audits in Amman, Beirut, and Cairo

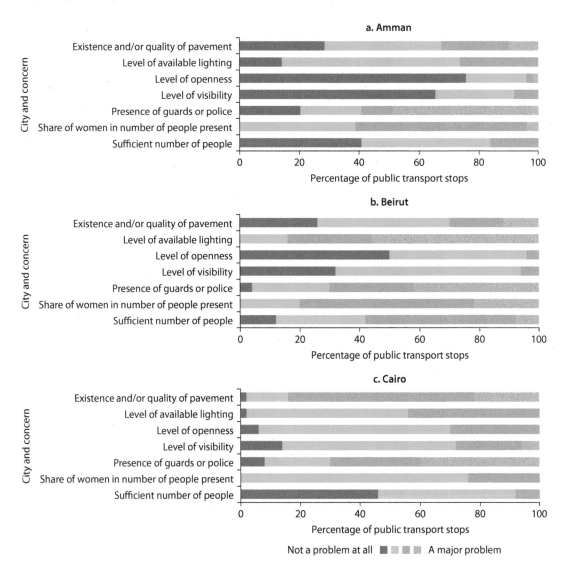

Source: Figure original to this publication using World Bank data: Built environment audits.

could vary by city, which is not observed in the data. Thus, the safety index should be considered an internal measure for each city, not a relative measure across cities. The results from the built environment surveys are combined to create a spatial index of safety based on the mean of the seven objective parameters with values from 0 (worse) to 100 percent (best)[15] (refer to map 3.3). These maps show an important difference in safety levels across each city.

MAP 3.3

Safety of Public Transport in Amman, Beirut, and Cairo

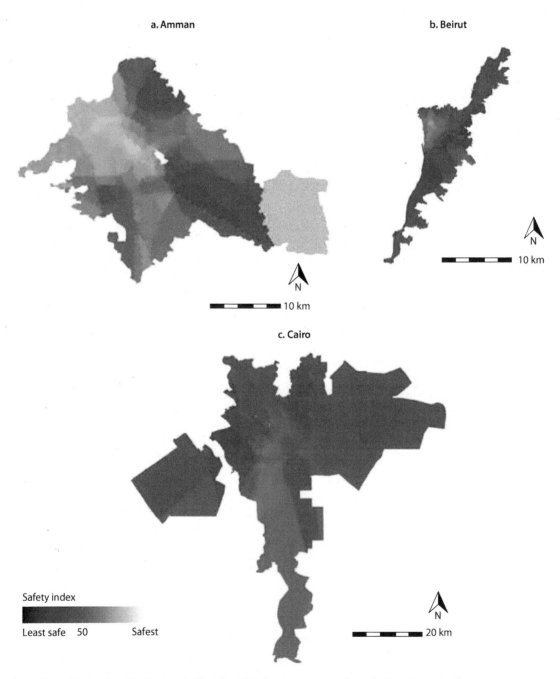

Source: Maps original to this publication based on World Bank data: Transit network mapping and built environment audits.

EFFECTS OF PUBLIC TRANSPORT ON LABOR MARKET OUTCOMES

Is a well-functioning[16] public transport system necessary for enhancing women's economic empowerment? On its own, is a well-functioning public transport system sufficient to significantly increase women's economic activity? This section examines the effect of three aspects of the public transport network on women's labor market outcomes in Amman, Beirut, and Cairo. In particular, it investigates how women's LFP and their likelihood of employment is affected by the accessibility of jobs throughout each city, the availability of public transport close to residential locations, and safety at or near public transport stops.[17] By doing so, this chapter illuminates whether improving public transport systems is a necessary or a sufficient condition for enhancing women's economic empowerment.

An empirical examination is performed to analyze whether spatial accessibility, availability, and safety of the public transport network affect women's labor market outcomes and whether there are differential effects of these transport measures by gender (refer to box 3.2). The spatial measures of accessibility, availability, and safety of the public transport network described in the previous section are matched with

---

BOX 3.2

Empirical Model Estimated

Two different models account for two types of labor market outcomes: labor force participation and the likelihood of having a job (employment probability).

The spatial accessibility, availability, and safety of the public transport network might affect the decision to participate in the labor market (having a job or being unemployed but looking for a job) versus not looking for a job. In this case, the analysis is restricted to women because much fewer working-age men are likely to be out of the labor force. Including men in the analysis to understand the likelihood of participating in the labor force would not be informative, because most are participating in the labor force.

The spatial accessibility, availability, and safety of the public transport network might also affect the likelihood of being employed. In this case, the analysis covers both men and women to assess whether transport affects employment probabilities among women and whether the effects are different by gender. For both these outcomes, the impact is calculated using a linear probability model to control for many individual, household, and geographic characteristics. Several tests and restrictions are used to ensure the robustness of the results.

the residential locations of the household survey respondents to estimate their effect on the labor market outcomes of individuals, using a linear probability model. The technical details of the empirical model can be found in Alam, Bagnoli, and Kerzhner (2023).[18] This section presents the main results of the empirical investigation along with the interpretation of these results.

The empirical analysis yields two broad findings (refer to figure 3.14). The first finding relates to women's LFP. The results show that a well-functioning public transport system is necessary for enhancing women's LFP. However, in each of the three cities, women's LFP is differently influenced or constrained by the three spatial measures of public transport quality (accessibility, availability, and safety). This finding implies that a one-size-fits-all-women approach to transport solutions is not appropriate, because women in the three cities face different binding constraints.

In addition, the constraints also appear to differ by income levels. These differences highlight the need for adopting an intersectional gender lens (refer to box 3.3). In Amman, safety appears to be the most important constraint that women face, while spatial accessibility to jobs is more important for women from low-income households (Alam et al. 2023). In Beirut, some evidence exists that spatial accessibility matters for women from low-income households. In Cairo, both accessibility and availability of public transport appear to play a strong role in determining women's LFP. The city-specific results and their implications are detailed as follows.

The second finding relates to men's and women's employment likelihood. While spatial accessibility, availability, and safety in public transport appear to affect women's likelihood of seeking a job, they have overall little impact on women's employment probability. In contrast, men's employment likelihood increases with improvements to the public transport system.

FIGURE 3.14

Main Results of the Empirical Analysis for This Study

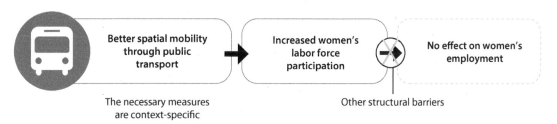

Source: Figure original to this publication based World Bank data.

Mobility, Access to Opportunities, and Intersectionality

The policies designed to benefit women may leave many of them behind if they are not viewed through an intersectional gender lens. Indeed, even within the same cultural or national context, some groups of women may enjoy more freedom of choice in making transport-related decisions than others. Intersecting gender with factors such as socioeconomic status, age, education, physical ability, or ethnicity can reveal many disparities among women within the same geographic area (Alam et al. 2022).

While many aspects of intersectionality are important to consider when designing transport policies, this report presents one aspect of intersectionality, namely the comparisons between women having low-income households with women overall.

The results imply that better spatial mobility through public transport is a necessary condition to increase women's LFP. However, improving public transport only is not sufficient without addressing the other structural, social, and family-related barriers. While a good public transport system improves women's participation in the labor force, it does not convert into actual employment, because that would depend on several supply- and demand-side factors such as demographic characteristics, education, and culture. These factors also include labor policy and labor market characteristics, such as the availability of jobs. Family-friendly workplace policies such as having day-care centers at or near places where people work or live or offering flexible work arrangements may also be beneficial.

Finally, a business culture that discriminates or segregates based on gender in the labor market can also be a contributing factor.[19] Thus, along with improving the accessibility, availability, and safety of public transport, policy measures that address work environment, social, and household constraints may be needed.

Results in Amman

In Amman, safety appears to be the most important constraint to women's LFP. Improving safety at or near public transport stops would significantly increase women's LFP. For instance, as illustrated in figure 3.15, in a scenario in which safety was to be improved by 5 percentage points (pp) (on average, this figure corresponds to increasing from an average score of 66 percent to 71 percent), the LFP among women would increase by 4.7 pp (from 13.6 to 18.3 percent of working-age women). In practice,

FIGURE 3.15

Impact of Increased Safety at Public Transport Stops on Women's LFP in Amman

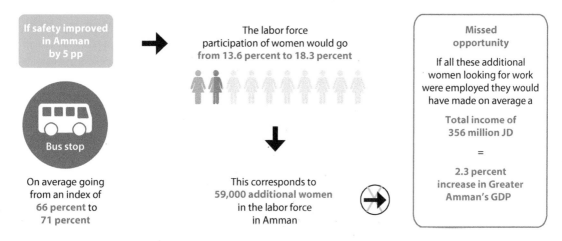

Source: Figure original to this publication using World Bank data.
Note: GDP = gross domestic product; JD = Jordanian dinar; LFP = labor force participation; pp = percentage points.

this figure corresponds to 59,000 additional women in the labor force in Amman. However, it does not translate to a significant improvement in employment probabilities and, therefore, is a missed opportunity for both women and the entire economy. If all the additional women looking for work were to find employment, it could lead to a total additional income of over JD (Jordanian dinar) 356 million per year,[20] equal to a 2.3 percent increase in Amman's gross domestic product (GDP).

However, although safety is the most important constraint among women overall, spatial accessibility appears to constrain women from lower-income households.[21] Among these women, the spatial accessibility of jobs is the most important constraint to LFP. A 5-pp increase in the share of jobs accessible within 60 minutes using public transport and walking would increase the LFP of women from lower-income households by 6.1 pp.

Results in Beirut

In Beirut, on average, no evidence exists that improving either spatial mobility measures would significantly improve women's LFP. This result is possibly due to the economic crisis that also creates many other barriers to the labor market. However, evidence exists that spatial accessibility matters for women from low-income households. Improving spatial mobility would not significantly improve women's LFP; however, among low-income women, an increase in the spatial accessibility of jobs through public transport by 5 pp would increase women's LFP by 3.7 pp.

Results in Cairo

In Cairo, both accessibility and availability of public transport appear to play an important role in determining women's LFP.[22] Improving the accessibility or availability of public transport in Cairo would significantly increase women's LFP. For instance, as illustrated in figure 3.16, in a scenario where accessibility was to be improved by 5 pp (on average, this figure corresponds to an increase from 13 percent of jobs accessible in less than 1 hour using public transport to 18 percent), the LFP among women in Cairo would increase by 4.9–8.9 pp, increasing from 19.1 percent to 23.9–27.9 percent of working-age women. In practice, this number corresponds to 337,000–614,000 additional women in the labor force in Cairo. However, this increase in LFP does not translate to a significant improvement in employment probabilities and is a missed opportunity for both women and the entire economy. If all the additional women seeking work were to find employment, it would lead to a total additional income of EGP (Egyptian pound) 12.4–22.7 billion per year,[23] and a 0.8–1.6 percent increase in Cairo's GDP. Improving the availability by 5 pp would increase women's LFP by 0.7 (corresponding to 52,000 additional women in the labor market).

The effects of improved accessibility and availability would be even bigger for women from low-income households. For instance, a 5-pp increase in accessibility would increase LFP among women in low-income households by 7.8–13.7 pp, and a 5-pp increase in availability would increase the LFP by 1 pp.

FIGURE 3.16

Impact of Increased Accessibility of Jobs through Public Transport on Women's LFP in Cairo

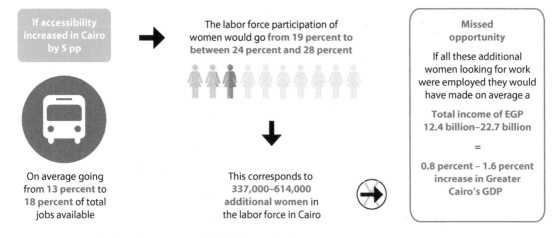

Source: Figure original to this publication using World Bank data.
Note: EGP = Egyptian pound; GDP = gross domestic product; LFP = labor force participation; pp = percentage points.

CONCLUSION

The findings of this chapter demonstrate that a deficient public transport system can inhibit women from being economically productive members of society. These results underscore that there is no one-size-fits-all solution for women and stress the importance of assessing the most important constraints in each context. These findings also highlight the importance of intersectionality and the need to consider that all women, even those within the same geographic context, might face different constraints. Finally, the results of this report indicate that merely focusing on transport is insufficient to improve women's access to economic empowerment. Other constraints, including gender norms, must be considered and interinstitutional collaboration encouraged. More precisely, the results of this chapter highlight many important messages.

Important differences exist in the commuting patterns of workers across cities. In Amman and Beirut, private vehicles constitute the main transport mode for commuters, while in Cairo, public transport is the main mode. Among those who use public transport to commute for work, microbuses are the most used in Amman and Cairo, while buses or minibuses are the most used in Beirut.

There is a "latent desire" to work among non-working women, and commuting is perceived as a barrier to work. In all three cities, most non-working women indicate that commuting is a barrier to working, but for differing reasons. Transport-related constraints dominate all three cities, but in Cairo, non–transport-related reasons play a larger role than in Amman or Beirut.

For transport-related constraints, women in Amman report the cost of commuting as the leading barrier to work, followed by the length of the trip. This finding flips in Cairo, where the length of trips is the most reported barrier, followed by the cost of commuting. In Beirut, the cost of commuting is the dominant constraint. For non–transport-related barriers to working, family preferences, domestic duties, and child-rearing pose a barrier to women working.

Spatial analysis reveals that the three cities exhibit varying levels of spatial accessibility to jobs by public transport and walking. Moreover, the distribution of spatial access to jobs is also highly unequal. Access to jobs through public transport and walking is the most unequal in Amman, followed by Cairo and Beirut.

Concerns about the safety of the built environment at public transport stops also vary across cities. In Amman and Cairo, the most salient issues are the absence or quality of pavement and sidewalks, while in Beirut, the lack of lighting at public transport stops is the most prevalent problem. Both aspects affect the safety of public transport stops. Moreover, in Amman and Beirut, there are fewer women at transport stations than in Cairo.

The empirical analysis confirms that a well-functioning public transport system is necessary for enhancing women's LFP, and the specific constraints differ by city and income levels. This analysis confirms that women's economic empowerment, through their LFP, is constrained by the quality of public transport according to its accessibility, availability, and safety. However, in each city, different constraints exist, which also differ by income levels. In Amman, safety appears to be the most important constraint that women face, while spatial accessibility to jobs is more important for women from low-income households. In Beirut, no evidence was found that improving spatial mobility would significantly improve women's LFP. This finding is possibly due to the economic crisis that also creates many other barriers to the labor market. However, evidence exists that spatial accessibility matters for women from low-income households. In Cairo, both the accessibility and availability of public transport appear to play a strong role in determining women's LFP, and their role is even larger for women from low-income households.

However, while accessibility, availability, and safety appear to affect, to varying degrees, women's likelihood of seeking a job, they seem to have little effect overall on women's subsequent employment probability. This finding is consistent with the idea that, while public transport can improve women's access to employment opportunities, making them more likely to actively seek jobs, complementary actions are needed to translate this active participation into gainful employment. This issue represents missed opportunities both for women and cities overall.

NOTES

1. Women are more likely than men to work in part-time, precarious, and flexible employment, and owing to the accompanying lower wages, are more sensitive to the cost of travel.
2. Based on 2022 data from the World Bank, World Development Indicators database.
3. For example, respondents have been found to systematically misreport commuting distances, especially in urban areas.
4. Methodological details on the construction of each indicator can be found in Alam, Bagnoli, and Kerzhner (2023).
5. Several assumptions needed to be made for using these data. The three cities have no pedestrian restrictions, meaning all streets and links in the network are considered accessible to pedestrians. It was assumed that a pedestrian walks at the speed of 3.6 km/h. A threshold of 20 minutes was set as the maximum walking time per leg of the trip when public transport is used. This restriction was chosen to reflect vulnerable and time-constrained mobility, which women often face.

6. This measure is based on a methodology developed by Barzin et al. (2022) using machine learning and remote sensing data.

7. Measures computed for the 8 am to 9 am window. A destination is considered reachable from a certain location if it can be reached in less than 60 minutes during at least 50 percent of the departures within the time window.

8. By definition and because of data availability, this measure accounts for the share of total jobs and not the number of actual jobs. Therefore, in larger cities such as Cairo, the share of jobs accessible from a certain location might be lower than in smaller cities, even when the number of jobs that are reachable is the same.

9. These accessibility levels are lower than those for many cities in developing countries where such analysis has been undertaken. Peralta-Quiros, Kerzhner, and Avner (2019) performed a benchmarking of 11 cities in Africa. Using this benchmarking, all three cities can be classified as the worst performers in connecting people with employment opportunities. Note that benchmarking data are available only for Africa.

10. The same assumptions were made as for the construction of the accessibility measure (no pedestrian restrictions, meaning all streets and links in the network are considered accessible to pedestrians and a pedestrian walking speed of 3.6 km/h).

11. This measure is computed between 8 am and 9 am in each city.

12. To normalize, the number of runs was divided by 60, and the values ≥1 were truncated to be equal to 100 percent. This standardization means the study presents an index of an average number of buses reachable each minute between 8 am and 9 am, at a maximum distance of a 10-minute walk, with the maximum being 1 bus per minute. At 1 bus per minute, the availability index equals 100 percent.

13. One stop in Amman was removed from the analysis during the data-cleaning phase because of strong outlier values.

14. These low levels can be explained by the long-lasting electricity and economic crisis in Lebanon, which has led the government to provide only 2 hours of public electricity per day.

15. Each location is assigned the average index of the 3 nearest surveyed stations.

16. Reliable, frequent, fast, comfortable, accessible, convenient, affordable, and safe.

17. Men are included for the employment probabilities to investigate whether there are heterogeneities by gender in the effect of the various aspects of transport. For LFP, this is not possible due to the high participation rates of men.

18. Also see Alam, Bagnoli, and Kerzhner (2023) for the limitations of the study in terms of both data collection and methodological approach.

19. It may also arise from a business culture at firms that do not value the contributions of female staff or that favor male employees to avoid providing maternity-related benefits or risking the loss of female employees after they are married.

20. Assuming they can earn the same as the prevalent average yearly income in the city (JD 6,077.59) with an inflation rate of 1.7 percent between 2020 and 2022 (Jordan News, 2022).

21. The lower-income group is defined for each city as the bottom half of the income distribution within the household survey sample.
22. Econometrically, only binding constraints could be assessed vis-à-vis labor market outcomes. This issue does not imply that non-binding constraints do not matter. For example, women could be braving or coping with unsafe conditions to access jobs in Cairo, which imposes a negative externality on them.
23. Assuming they can earn the same as the prevalent average yearly income in the city (EGP 36,902.58) with an inflation rate of 10.5 percent between 2020 and 2022 (El-Sayed, 2023).

REFERENCES

Alam, M. M., L. Bagnoli, and T. Kerzhner. 2023. "The ABCs of the Role of Public Transport in Women's Economic Empowerment." Policy Research Working Paper 10404, World Bank, Washington, DC. http://hdl.handle.net/10986/39682.

Alam, M. M., N. Kurshitashvili, K. Dominguez Gonzalez, K. Gonzalez Carvajal, and B. Baruah. 2022. *Is a Mile for One a Mile for All? A Knowledge Synthesis Report on Gender and Mobility (2000–20)*. Washington, DC: World Bank. doi:10.1596/37354.

Alhawarin, I., N. Berri, I. Selwaness, and M. Sieverding. 2020. "The Care Economy in Jordan: Towards Recognizing, Reducing and Redistributing Unpaid Care Work." Policy Brief No. 3, UN Women, New York. https://arabstates.unwomen.org/sites/default/files/Field%20Office%20Arab%20States/Attachments/Publications/2020/12/English_PolicyBrief_Jordan.pdf.

Aloul, S., R. Naffa, and M. Mansour. 2018. *Gender in Public Transportation: A Perspective of Women Users of Public Transportation*. SADAQA, Friedrich-Ebert-Stiftung, Amman, Jordan.

Barzin, S., P. Avner, J. Rentschler, and N. O'Clery. 2022. "Where Are All the Jobs? A Machine Learning Approach for High Resolution Urban Employment Prediction in Developing Countries." Policy Research Working Paper 9979, World Bank, Washington, DC. doi:10.1596/1813-9450-9979.

Bastiaanssen, J., D. Johnson, and K. Lucas. 2020. "Does Transport Help People to Gain Employment? A Systematic Review and Meta-Analysis of the Empirical Evidence." *Transport Reviews* 40 (5): 607–28. doi:10.1080/01441647.2020.1747569.

El-Sayed, R. 2023 "Equal Pay Day in Egypt: Addressing the Gender Wage Gap Crisis." *El-Shai*, March 14, 2023. https://www.el-shai.com/equal-pay-day-in-egypt-gender-wage-gap-crisis/#:~:text=Women%20in%20Egypt%20%20earn%20significantly,gender%20wage%20gap%20of%2034.9%25.

Jordan News. 2022. "Average monthly salary of Jordanian workers is JD543." *Jordan News*, December 13, 2022. https://www.jordannews.jo/Section-109/News/Average-monthly-salary-of-Jordanian-workers-is-JD543-25687.

Peralta-Quiros, T., T. Kerzhner, and P. Avner. 2019. "Exploring Accessibility to Employment Opportunities in African Cities: A First Benchmark." Policy

Research Working Paper 8971, World Bank, Washington, DC. https://papers.ssrn.com/abstract=3434753.

Redaelli, S., A. Lnu, S. P. Buitrago Hernandez, and T. Ismail. 2023. *State of the Mashreq Women Flagship: Who Cares? Care Work and Women's Labor Market Outcomes in Iraq, Jordan, and Lebanon (English)*. Washington, DC: World Bank. https://documents1.worldbank.org/curated/en/099000502222338765/pdf/P16815701c336d00e095dc093ef29af40a7.pdf.

Selwaness, I., and I. Helmy. 2020. "The Care Economy in Egypt: The Road Towards Recognizing, Reducing and Redistributing Unpaid Care Work." Policy Brief No. 2, UN Women, New York. https://arabstates.unwomen.org/sites/default/files/Field%20Office%20Arab%20States/Attachments/Publications/2020/12/UNW_ERF_PolicyBriefs_Egypt_final_Dec4_2020.pdf.

United Nations. 2019. *Why Addressing Women's Income and Time Poverty Matters for Sustainable Development*. World Survey on the Role of Women in Development, UN Women, New York. https://www.unwomen.org/sites/default/files/Headquarters/Attachments/Sections/Library/Publications/2019/World-survey-on-the-role-of-women-in-development-2019.pdf.

CHAPTER 4

Recommendations

INTRODUCTION

The evidence presented throughout this publication demonstrates that a well-functioning public transport system is necessary to improve women's economic participation in the labor market. Thus, the costs of not improving public transport for women are high. Even in a scenario where all other constraints to women's access to employment were removed, the existing quality of public transport in urban Middle East and North Africa (MENA) would not allow women to reach employment opportunities and would impede them from fully gaining employment.

This chapter provides concrete recommendations for improving women's mobility and economic participation. The first section highlights the actions needed to improve the public transport system in all three cities, which are relevant to both women and men. Because the evidence in this report has highlighted that "one size does not fit all women," the second section provides the most important actions needed in each city to improve women's mobility. The third section identifies the necessary improvements to the public transport system in each city that would result in the increased participation of women in the labor force. In some instances, actions may be recommended to address multiple issues and thus are repeated. Finally, because this report also highlights that while improving public transport is a necessary condition to improve women's economic participation in the labor market, it is not a sufficient one, and so the fourth section presents the complementary actions needed in other sectors to transform a higher labor force participation (LFP) among women that develops into gainful employment.

WHAT CONCRETE ACTIONS ARE NEEDED TO IMPROVE THE PUBLIC TRANSPORT SYSTEMS IN ALL THREE CITIES?

This report demonstrates that, across all cities, there are low and unequal levels of accessibility to jobs through public transport and walking, as well as a low availability of public transport near residential locations. This issue highlights the need for the following concrete actions:

- Those that enhance the coverage of the public transport network, including improving the feeder network, prioritizing public transport through integrated corridor management or the creation of or improvements to mass transit (like bus rapid transit or metro trains), increasing the frequency of service, rethinking the placement of existing public transport stops, and supporting a supply-and-demand analysis and new routes based on demand.

- Those that enhance the walkability of the cities, including improving sidewalks and walkways and developing pedestrian-first policies.

- Those that improve existing land regulations to foster dense, diverse, and well-designed urban developments.

In all three cities, the cost of public transport poses a major barrier to women commuting to work. This issue emphasizes the need to address the affordability of the public transport system with the following concrete actions:

- Lowering the cost of using public transport or offering targeted fare concessions. Targeted fares could rely on a combination of sociodemographic factors (such as gender, age, or income level) so as not to jeopardize the financial sustainability of public transport systems.

- Developing other ways to reduce the total cost of travel. This reduction in the total cost of transport could be accomplished through integrated fares for trips requiring more than one means of transport or day passes for those who need to travel many times during the day.

WHAT CONCRETE AND CITY-SPECIFIC ACTIONS ARE NEEDED TO IMPROVE WOMEN'S MOBILITY?

Surveys of public transport users demonstrate that women face distinct challenges with public transport usage in each city. This section identifies improvements to public transport and the cities in which they constitute a major barrier to women. For each aspect, recommendations are made that would enhance the experience of women who already use public transport. These concrete actions also could attract additional women into the public transport system, which is important, because women remain an under-represented rider segment. The recommended concrete actions are as follows:

- Those that improve the comfort of trips are particularly important in Amman and Beirut. These actions can be classified into two groups. First are actions that can increase the overall comfort of the riding environment, such as those related to the ease of use of public transport when traveling with children, with heavy bags or belongings, or with reduced physical mobility, as well as those addressing overcrowded vehicles to provide safer environments for women. Second are actions such as creating or improving the waiting areas around public transport stops, as well as providing bathroom facilities at certain stops to improve comfort.[1]

- Actions that decrease the total travel time by public transport are particularly important in Amman and Cairo. Decreasing both total travel and waiting times at bus stops is important for women in these two cities. Actions that increase network coverage, service frequency, and connectivity between transport means—can decrease travel and waiting times between means of transport. Other actions cover enhancing certainty about arrival and departure times, as well as strengthening confidence in the safety of the public transport locations.

- Actions that increase the affordability of public transport could benefit women in all three cities. Affordability is a constraint to women already using public transport in Beirut and Cairo.

- Actions that improve road safety are particularly important in Beirut. These actions relate to many other transport aspects, including the quality of roads and infrastructure, the quality and maintenance of public transport vehicles, and the driving behaviors of public transport drivers and other drivers in general.

- Actions that improve pavement and sidewalks are particularly important in Amman and Cairo. These types of actions should address both the presence and quality of walking pathways and pavements to transport stops.

- Actions to improve the lighting at transport stops are particularly important in Beirut, where most of the audited public transport stops did not have adequate levels of lighting at night.

WHAT CONCRETE ACTIONS ARE NEEDED TO IMPROVE WOMEN'S ECONOMIC PARTICIPATION THROUGH BETTER PUBLIC TRANSPORT?

In analyzing how the accessibility, availability, and safety of public transport systems can affect women's LFP, this report demonstrates that a well-functioning public transport system is needed to enhance women's economic empowerment. However, the specific constraints vary by city.

In Amman, safety appears to be the most important constraint to women's overall LFP, while spatial accessibility is the largest barrier for women from lower-income households. Improving the safety around public transport stops would significantly increase women's LFP, which would lead to significant gains in gross domestic product (GDP) if all women in the labor market were to find employment. Providing a safe environment for women to access public transport includes actions such as well-lit and visible stops and better walkways and bicycle paths. It also requires a code of conduct for public transport drivers and an easy mechanism to report gender-based violence, as well as to receive a swift response to these reports. For example, Jordan adopted a code of conduct for public transport in January 2019, as well as a mobile phone application for the code of conduct, called *Muwasalati*, that enables bus riders to report misconduct in public transport systems. These are important steps toward improving safety and enhancing the perception of safety.

In Beirut, evidence suggests that spatial accessibility matters for women from low-income households. Thus, actions that improve the accessibility to jobs in economically poorer areas would be beneficial.

In Cairo, both accessibility and availability of public transport appear to play an important role in determining women's LFP. The effects would be even more significant for women from low-income households. Hence, all actions that would result in an increase in the availability or accessibility of public transport systems would lead to a significant increase in women's LFP and important potential gains in GDP if all women seeking employment were to find employment.

Across all cities, the results of the empirical analysis underscore the importance of examining mobility and gender through an intersectional lens. Indeed, improving accessibility and availability to public transport can yield significant economic gains.

COMPLEMENTARY RECOMMENDATIONS IN OTHER SECTORS

Along with improving the affordability, accessibility, availability, and safety of public transport, policy measures addressing constraints in work, social, and household environments, as well as norms and expectations about gender roles, are needed to transform higher LFP among women into gainful employment.

For gender norms and cultural barriers in general, actions that would change the expectations for women to shoulder household responsibilities and for the division of unpaid care and domestic work could increase women's opportunities to find paid work outside of the household. Other barriers include the low social acceptance of women in the workforce and challenges related to mixed-gender workplaces (Arab Barometer 2023). Raising awareness and conveying messages that can contribute to changing attitudes and behaviors toward the role of women within society and their use of public transport can help address cultural barriers.

For actions related to labor markets and work environments, there is a need to provide flexible work arrangements and to support jobs that would allow women to balance their personal, family, and work lives. Moreover, a business culture that discriminates based on gender and prioritizes men over women in the workplace can cause low economic participation among women.

The lack of childcare options is often cited as a significant barrier to workplace entry by women in MENA (Arab Barometer 2023). Therefore, family-friendly workplace policies such as high-quality daycare centers at or near places where people work and live may be beneficial and could have a significant impact on women's ability to access employment.

Overall, this evidence supports the need for intersectoral and inter-institutional collaboration to address the multifaceted challenges and barriers faced by women on their path toward greater economic empowerment. In this context, multisectoral committees and advisory groups can play a pivotal role in addressing not only transport-related barriers but also other obstacles to women's employment.

NOTE

1. Gender-informed restrooms at transport stops should have twice as many stalls for women than those in the men's restrooms.

REFERENCE

Arab Barometer. 2023. *MENA Women in the Workforce 2022—Wave VII.* 2022 Arab Barometer Insight. https://www.arabbarometer.org/2023/02/mena -women-in-the-workforce/.